Centre for Educational Research and Innovation (CERI)

ONE SCHOOL,
MANY CULTURES

ORGANISATION FOR ECONOMIC CO-OPERATION AND DEVELOPMENT

Pursuant to article 1 of the Convention signed in Paris on 14th December 1960, and which came into force on 30th September 1961, the Organisation for Economic Co-operation and Development (OECD) shall promote policies designed:

- to achieve the highest sustainable economic growth and employment and a rising standard of living in Member countries, while maintaining financial stability, and thus to contribute to the development of the world economy;
- to contribute to sound economic expansion in Member as well as non-member countries in the process of economic development; and
- to contribute to the expansion of world trade on a multilateral, non-discriminatory basis in accordance with international obligations.

The original Member countries of the OECD are Austria, Belgium, Canada, Denmark, France, the Federal Republic of Germany, Greece, Iceland, Ireland, Italy, Luxembourg, the Netherlands, Norway, Portugal, Spain, Sweden, Switzerland, Turkey, the United Kingdom and the United States. The following countries became Members subsequently through accession at the dates indicated hereafter: Japan (28th April 1964), Finland (28th January 1969), Australia (7th June 1971) and New Zealand (29th May 1973).

The Socialist Federal Republic of Yugoslavia takes part in some of the work of the OECD (agreement of 28th October 1961).

The Centre for Educational Research and Innovation was created in June 1968 by the Council of the Organisation for Economic Co-operation and Development for an initial period of three years, with the help of grants from the Ford Foundation and the Royal Dutch Shell Group of Companies. Since May 1971, the Council has periodically extended the mandate, which now expires on 31st December 1991.

The main objectives of the Centre are as follows:

- *to promote and support the development of research activities in education and undertake such research activities where appropriate;*
- *to promote and support pilot experiments with a view to introducing and testing innovations in the educational system;*
- *to promote the development of co-operation between Member countries in the field of educational research and innovation.*

The Centre functions within the Organisation for Economic Co-operation and Development in accordance with the decisions of the Council of the Organisation, under the authority of the Secretary-General. It is supervised by a Governing Board composed of one national expert in its field of competence from each of the countries participating in its programme of work.

Publié en français sous le titre :

L'ÉCOLE
ET LES CULTURES

This volume presents and examines the results of the Secretariat's analysis of educational programmes that have been conducted in a number of countries as a response to the multicultural, multiethnic and multilingual nature of contemporary societies.

It has been prepared as part of the CERI project of enquiry into Education and the Cultural and Linguistic Pluralism (ECALP) which was built around two issues: the education of immigrants' children, and multicultural education policies. The first of these has been covered in the report *Immigrants' children at school* (1987); the second is the subject of the present publication.

The study is directed primarily at specialists in multicultural education, and policy–makers in the whole field of education. For this reason, it does not include a description of any specific programme of multicultural education implemented at any particular school. What it attempts, rather, is to clarify the present trends in multicultural education and to portray the reactions of the educational system under the pressure of cultural and linguistic development, as reflected in the experiences and policies of Member countries.

The issues treated here are as conceptually difficult as they are politically complex and sensitive; the report does not, therefore, pretend to do more than provide a clarifying basis on which the debate around these problems can be pursued, recognising the widely differing views and situations that exist between Member countries as well as within the countries themselves. This report has been prepared by Mr. Norberto Bottani, of the CERI Secretariat. Notable comments have also been made by several consultants whose contributions improved the various drafts of this study.

J.R. Gass
Director
Centre for Educational
Research and Innovation

Also available

MULTICULTURAL EDUCATION (September 1987)
(96 87 03 1) ISBN 92-64-12989-8   350 pages   £12.00   US$25.00   FF120.00   DM52.00

IMMIGRANTS' CHIDREN AT SCHOOL (May 1987)
(96 87 02 1) ISBN 92-64-12954-5   322 pages   £12.00   US$22.00   FF120.00   DM44.00

THE FUTURE OF MIGRATION (May 1987)
(81 87 01 1) ISBN 92-64-12949-9   320 pages   £10.00   US$20.00   FF100.00   DM44.00

EDUCATION AND TRAINING AFTER BASIC SCHOOLING (August 1985)
(91 85 03 1) ISBN 92-64-12742-9   132 pages   £8.00   US$16.00   FF80.00   DM35.00

EDUCATION IN MODERN SOCIETY (July 1985)
(91 85 02 1) ISBN 92-64-12739-9   108 pages   £7.00   US$14.00   FF70.00   DM31.00

MIGRANTS' CHILDREN AND EMPLOYMENT. The European Experience (May 1983)
(81 83 02 1) ISBN 92-64-12434-9   64 pages   £4.00   US$8.00   FF40.00   DM16.00

Prices charged at the OECD Bookshop.

*THE OECD CATALOGUE OF PUBLICATIONS and supplements will be sent free of charge
on request addressed either to OECD Publications Service,
2, rue André-Pascal, 75775 PARIS CEDEX 16, or to the OECD Distributor in your country.*

CONTENTS

Introduction 7

Chapter I. **The lines of investigation** 13

    Cultural identity 16
    Greater cultural uniformity 17
    Cultural relativism 18
    The new minorities 19
    Multilingual contexts 20
    The ethnic dilemma 21
    Notes and references 22

Chapter II. **The multicultural context** 23

    The socio–geographical context 23
    The urban changes 26
    The terminological misunderstandings 27
    Notes and references 31

Chapter III. **Multicultural education policies in the OECD countries** 35

    Sweden 36
    Finland 37
    United Kingdom 38
        England 38
        Wales 40
        Scotland 40
    Ireland 41
    Spain 42
    Italy 45
    Yugoslavia 46
    New Zealand 47
    Australia 48
    Canada 50
    United States 53
    Notes and references 54

Chapter IV. **Issues in the debate on multicultural education** 57

    The social consensus 59
    The cultural identity 60
    Competences of the education system and multicultural reality 63
    The limits to multicultural education policies 66
    Weaknesses of the theoretical framework 68
    Notes and references 70

Chapter V. **Conclusions** 73
    Notes and references 79

INTRODUCTION

Our subject is a delicate one, especially for an international organisation, which must not run the risk of interfering in countries' internal affairs. In order to avoid being accused of such interference and the opposite danger of giving stereotyped banal explanations, we have preferred to focus more on cognitive issues than on legal problems. The guiding concern has been to identify and clarify the nature and origin of the concepts used by policy–makers in multicultural education. The term "multicultural education" is a convenient one and we shall use it frequently, but it must be said at the outset that this report is not concerned with such education *per se* but with the implications of cultural and linguistic pluralism for education.

This approach will perhaps disappoint militant champions of the lesser known languages and cultures who are fighting to improve the living conditions and status of minority communities. Thus, the report does not offer any solutions to very real and in some cases very old problems such as those relating to the rights of cultural and linguistic minorities. The theme of the present analysis is the challenge that cultural relativism poses for education as it has developed in contemporary democratic societies. The intention of this report is above all to stimulate enquiry into issues that have been more or less overlooked in the discussion on the development of multicultural education.

Two topics constantly reappear in most publications on multicultural education: familiarity with other cultures (a subject which examines the possibility of getting to know these through the school and also raises the question of the meaning of receptiveness to new cultures) and language teaching.

On familiarity with other cultures, those who recommend extending multicultural education or developing intercultural education usually agree that most curricula are ethnocentric and that one way of obtaining real understanding and mutual tolerance between the members of the different communities is by relativising these curricula, pruning them and including lessons on other cultures. It is hoped that by getting pupils to realise that there are other ways of thinking, they will learn that their own culture is not intrinsically superior, nor others necessarily inferior. It is nonetheless curious to see how this idea of opening pupils' minds to other cultures and the mentality and practices of minority groups has been put into effect. We are not for the moment discussing the theoretical grounds for attacking the ethnocentric orientation of curricula. What we would like to point out here is the fact that most of the multicultural curricula offered in schools (particularly in the European countries) are targeted at the "others" and only concern pupils from the ethnic minority communities instead of the whole school population.

There is, however, one exception to this general rule: the intercultural approach. Its aim is ambitious: to form a new open cultural identity which is neither Eurocentric nor ethnocentric, nor passionately tied to its own beliefs and values. The problem of ethnocentrism is one of the main issues in this debate, from the political as well as the ethical and cognitive standpoints. It therefore deserves much closer attention since it cannot be minimised or solved by wishful thinking or moralising.

Language teaching is the other main topic in discussions on multicultural education since conflicts about language exacerbate the confrontation between majority and minority ethnic groups. The fierce defence of languages becomes meaningful if we do not disguise the fact that the real issue is not only linguistic but also political, not to say economic. Yet discussions on education tend to conceal this dimension, which is mainly glimpsed via the efforts to cure linguistic difficulties by purely educational means.

It is entirely understandable that in educational circles the multicultural issue should have become centred around language, for modern schools have become institutions with a mission to standardize language. The school has always been the shrine of language, so to speak. In endeavouring to inculcate and enforce linguistic standards, the school has been performing a cultural and a social function: it has been engaged in the work of linguistic unification demanded by economic development in industrial society and it has established the criteria for social selection, which are based on the language skills acquired at school.

Turning to multicultural education programmes in the different countries, we are struck by the similarities of the policy measures proposed and the extreme variety of cultural situations. How much flexibility can there be, therefore, in policies for multicultural education given the kaleidoscope of interests that must be taken into account, if one accepts the principle that the school must adapt to its environment and respect the characteristics of local communities? The ethnic, cultural and linguistic diversity found in modern cities is a major problem for the education authorities. What should they do? Increase the number of projects, schemes and programmes to allow for the cultural and linguistic diversity of the school population? Reject special educational measures for minority groups, consider other alternatives or do nothing at all?

At school level, the situation is rather bleak: the available programmes are inadequate for needs, the quality of courses is sometimes dubious and ethnic groups are not all treated in the same way, some receiving constant attention while others are neglected. The situation is no better when we turn from practice to theory.

The analysis of factors that constitute the reasons and justifications for multicultural education is unsoundly based, uncertain and narrow in scope, and inevitably encourages a drift into folklore and moralising.

Yet cultural practices are not merely valuable as subjects for museum exhibitions or ethnology lectures. Their continuing existence indicates, as de Certeau[1] suggests, that within the market economy there are systems of exchange, forms of solidarity and usages which are determined by a different economic logic based on other rules. Immersed deeply in the social organism, they preserve different forms of organising and utilising space, time, social relations, exchanges and knowledge.

These different cultural practices which are mainly apparent through the behaviour, beliefs and forms of social organisation of ethnic groups and immigrant communities exist side by side with the uniform, stereotyped practices and lifestyles imposed by the economic evolution of advanced industrial society. This coexistence is part of a complex process: people move from one system to another and exchanges take place between different systems of values; osmosis occurs, but not necessarily fusion. Since differences persist despite contact and mutual influence, the cultural practices of ethnic groups repeat within the relatively advanced system of social relations and values of developed industrial society a diversity (though we might call it density or depth) which helps to preserve or establish a whole range of forms of socialisation, mutual help, solidarity and personal development which are extremely rewarding for community life.

To demonstrate the interweaving between majority and minority cultures in contemporary multicultural societies De Certeau uses the term "minor" in its musical sense. In the same way that a minor mode differs from the major mode without excluding it, there are also minor cultures and minor economies. Minor does not mean inferior. It signifies a different way of life, a different form of sociality and community membership, a different key. The kind of opposition that exists between dominant and dominated, between majority and minority, does not exist between major and minor.

In one way or another, the sociality of ethnic groups refers to community experience which is far from being exclusively cultural. According to de Certeau, "migrants or the members of so—called minority groups reintroduce into an administration (legal, economic or educational) based on individual rights, the rights of communities, which cannot be reduced to the sum of their individual members. By virtue of a language, a body of practices or a common history, a social entity exists over and above the variants presented by its members, and it is on this basis that they demand recognition"[2]. Preserving and protecting minority cultures is not therefore just a question of special action at the level of the school and does not only depend upon the introduction of more or less enlightened policies.

The dynamics of the development and reproduction of the cultures which we have agreed here to call "minor" is only partly influenced by that governing the dominant cultures. Yet the latter refer to their own categories to codify behaviour, mentalities, languages and ways of thinking that they do not share. Great care and very subtle analysis are therefore called for in order to get to know, study and compare them, as de Certeau very aptly pointed out:

"First of all, a considerable part of what we regard as 'cultural' — or which we have transformed into 'cultural' expressions and activities — corresponds to those areas of social life that the individualistic assumptions of our analytical and management structures have made incomprehensible to us in economic terms. We call 'cultural' those configurations or fragments of economies which obey other criteria than our own. The word identifies within a different group (or in our own) what we can now only think of as exotic manifestations, symbolic structures or customary practices not amenable to the law of the market."[3].

This comment should be a warning to anyone who juggles with culture in the schools. The school often displays manifestations of cultural minorities in the form of cultural relics, through language and culture or history and geography lessons. By failing to understand that these are signs, or a kind of lexicon, of older forms of solidarity or conviviality, the schools may then drain these symbols of their substance and, indeed, their rationality.

We mentioned that there is a certain correlation between economic crises and the revival of ethnic and regionalist movements. This is understandable in the light of what we have just said concerning "minor" cultures. It is not surprising that in periods of crisis there should be an upsurge in ethnic values: when an economic system is in turmoil, these values act as signposts which help people to find support, assistance and at the very least an identity. The popularity of multicultural curricula probably reflects this situation.

A similar interpretation can, moreover, be given for a concomitant though inverse development, namely the attenuation of ethnic demands when the economic situation worsens. While higher unemployment, lower purchasing power and harsh competition on the labour market can foster a compensatory interest in ethnic values, they also damp down cultural clashes. During an economic downturn, finding a job, security of employment, doing well at school and integrating in social life become priorities. The crisis thus both prompts and attenuates ethnic demands. We must therefore be careful given the emergence of political and educational movements that focus on the problems of cultural and linguistic difference.

First of all, we must examine the significance of the "cultural" label put on certain kinds of conduct and practices. Classing these as cultural objects is not an innocuous operation. Calling any object a cultural object is in itself problematical. Next, we must not forget that beneath the cultural uniformity of advanced industrial society there are social practices, domestic lifestyles, forms of solidarity and thinking, and beliefs which function according to other codes and symbols. Lastly, the fluctuation of political and cultural interests around ethnic cultures (well illustrated by the concept of "revival") must also be considered. The need for attachment to beliefs and values which is demonstrated through the use and defence of little–spoken languages or dying dialects reveals people's deeper yearning for values and firm anchor points in order to build themselves an identity, feel secure and enjoy life. It is normal that this need should be perceived more or less intensely in the light of political and economic circumstances, and it is not surprising that it can be manipulated in many ways. For this reason, the hardening of ethnic interests and the way cultural differences are perceived as problems must be examined in the light of socio–political developments.

How should the problem of cultural difference be viewed today in schools? What has been done so far to "open" the minds of pupils (the metaphor is interesting and would merit discussion) to other cultures and to get students to accept lifestyles different from their own and if possible to understand them? What results have been obtained where curricula have been modified in the direction of intercultural education? Has any serious evaluation been made of these innovations? What role can the State school play in preserving the cultural values and traditions of a minority ethnic community and what skills can the school count on to carry out such a task efficiently?

More attention must be paid to these critical issues. Practice in multicultural education has often taken precedence over conceptual clarification and the preparation of a valid theoretical framework. But no significant progress can be made in future in multicultural education if the basic questions are not put frankly and with strict theoretical rectitude. The debate on this point is not closed as the problems raised by the development of multicultural education are extremely complex. What is involved is the very concept of the nature of knowledge and its organisation, that of science, and the way every society sees itself and its relations with others and the rest of the world.

The report is in five parts:

— Chapter I describes the genesis and purpose of the CERI project of enquiry, its terms of reference and aims, and outlines the documentation on which it has been based;

— In Chapter II, we describe the main features of the socio–cultural changes produced by the recent ethnic explosion which has transformed the social landscape in a good many Member countries, and we attempt to clarify terminological difficulties which tend to distort discussions about multicultural education;

— Chapter III sets out the approaches taken by Member countries to tackle the cultural changes described. Comparisons then bring out a number of shared key problems and help to identify the direction of current developments in the OECD area;

— Chapter IV analyses the principal problems revealed by the comparison of multicultural education policies;

— The final chapter draws conclusions from this analysis, which is intended to give the clearest possible formulation of the problems to be overcome. The future orientation of multicultural education policies will indeed be substantially influenced by the way in which the multicultural issue is stated.

To conclude this introduction, we must point out that, given the subject and countries' reluctance to discuss it at international level, we had to confine the field of analysis to observing how cultural and linguistic differences are perceived nowadays in education policy. Rather than giving detailed descriptions of multicultural education programmes (which is adequately done in the abundant documentation for the Council of Europe project on education and cultural development of migrants, in the European Commission's papers on the education of migrants' children and in various publications on multicultural education that will be listed in the notes as the report proceeds), we have preferred to look at the purpose of these programmes and the goals of the agencies that produced them. This report is mainly concerned with the issues underlying the preparation of multicultural education programmes. By analysing the complex fabric of interests and forces which determine the range of variations that these programmes may include, a better understanding will be obtained of the education policies introduced to cope with ethnic diversity.

It should also be noted that, before any analysis is made of educational systems, there is a need for a more exhaustive examination of three major problems raised by the cultural and linguistic diversity of the populations of most OECD countries. The first concerns the integration in developed societies of ethnic communities which have their own language and culture, allowing for the variety of possible situations: "regional" communities made minorities by the national construction of the different countries, transfrontier communities and communities formed by both older and more recent immigrations. Governments must consider ways of integrating these various minorities with a view to redefining their own general policy in this connection.

Education policy should normally stem from this updating of the life of the different communities in a given national framework. The word updating is the right one. In a single country there are often highly contradictory realities which cannot be coherently translated into the educational systems: the nationalism which led to the building of a State in the past still exists, for example, side by side with new attitudes that open the way for the integration of minorities whose specific cultural and linguistic differences are respected. The opening–up attempts made by multicultural education in such contradictory situations are soon perceived as a front and the progress claimed is rejected by the populations concerned.

The same applies to problems concerning the connection between minority situations and economic and social inequality. Here again, the school may be in a divisive position since multicultural education can become a mere front or, on the contrary, a truly effective weapon against inequality.

Lastly, there is the question of cultural relativism. This is a major issue which would merit a lengthy study on its own account. Clearly, if this fundamental research is not carried out, we must inevitably either minimise real cultural differences or confine the different cultures in as many ghettos and speak about cultural incommunicability. If education is to allow for cultural and linguistic pluralism, we must build a new picture of rationality.

The report's conclusions endeavour to show how to throw off Manichean attitudes (ethnocentric universalism, on the one side, and epistemological indifference, on the other) in order to explore the possibility of teaching adapted to a contemporary society which is typified by the coexistence of different cultures.

NOTES AND REFERENCES

1. De Certeau, M.: "The Management of Ethnic Resources: Schooling for Diversity", in *Multicultural education*. OECD/CERI, Paris, 1987.
2. *Ibid.*, p. 170.
3. *Ibid.*, p. 170.

Chapter I

THE LINES OF INVESTIGATION

This report draws heavily, as background, on a series of papers prepared for an ECALP symposium by a selected group of experts in the field of linguistic and cultural pluralism. They are acknowledged by name in the text that follows and the papers themselves (here developed in a more political perspective) are printed in Multicultural Education *published by the OECD recently.*

For an intergovernmental agency concerned with economics such as the OECD to take an interest in minority ethnic groups is not exactly the norm and it is legitimate to ask how international co-operation can contribute to settling problems raised by the presence of minorities within given countries. Throughout the centuries governments have jealously barred this field from outside interference and even today a sort of conditioned reflex operates against bringing the issue of national minorities into the international stage for discussion with representatives of other governments.

Additionally, recent socio-economic developments, the results of equal-opportunity policies in education, the changes in migratory flows and the popularity of a world-wide culture disseminated at an astonishing pace by the media, are altering the position of minorities or at least the way in which their situation is seen or represented. It was relatively straightforward to deal with minorities when they were stable and occupied a specific territory; it is far less simple when these communities move, cross frontiers, expand or shrink, and interact with each other. Distinctions become blurred, and a new terminology emerges ("new minorities"; "non-territorial minorities") to describe situations that lie outside any traditional pattern.

No country is exempt from such changes, which generate hybrid cultural, legal, economic and educational situations that are difficult to control and which call for new and different policies. The similarity of problems and the lack of precedents then open up prospects for international co-operation, which may be especially relevant when attention is confined to educational questions. Children from minority ethnic groups are over-represented among low achievers everywhere. Educational reforms of recent decades have not noticeably improved their chances of success.

Before co-operative international activity could be accepted and taken up, however, there was a need for a different perception of the educational problems of children from outside the dominant cultural groups, and for a non-nationalist approach to educational objectives. A meeting ground became apparent once inequalities and low educational achievement began to be interpreted using a cultural and social paradigm to explain differences without referring in any way to political consideration.

Towards the end of the 1970s CERI started to look, quite indirectly, at matters relating to multicultural education as part of a project on the funding, organisation and administration of schooling for special groups. Linguistic and indigenous minorities were among the categories considered: the scale and number of programmes for them in fact warranted a special review, conducted with the help of a number of countries. The special report on this activity[1], comparing procedures for applying educational programmes for linguistic and cultural minorities, revealed a surprising consistency across the programmes and showed steps and stages that are found in all the multicultural education policies observed.

This central finding was a decisive step in the analysis of multicultural education policies. Two of the guiding principles in this report stem directly from it. The first principle is the possibility of a predictive theory of multicultural education, i.e. one that will predict fairly accurately the development of multicultural education policies in individual national contexts. If the theory holds true (something any scientific work aims at), it will allow prediction and control of the impact of particular measures. It will then be possible to take non–random decisions.

The second guiding principle is the morphogenetic nature of multicultural education: its development would appear to be affected more by the laws governing education systems than by cultural, social and economic factors outside education. It should not be deduced from this, however, that the genesis of multicultural education programmes is only determined by the institutional environment. When examining definitions of multicultural education policy objectives, in fact, Churchill shows that the chief factor involved in formulating them is majority public opinion, which in turn is determined by a relatively straightforward and explicit typology of the perceived educational problems of cultural and linguistic minorities. In addition, a detailed survey of the conditions that have allowed multicultural education to emerge brings out clearly the influence of the political and economic context.

The country reports that the CERI Secretariat requested at the outset of the ECALP project from those Member countries which had expressed a readiness to discuss and compare multicultural education policy confirmed the validity of this thesis[2]. All the reports stressed that the choice of options had been dictated by a political strategy extending beyond the educational sphere.

The documents showed a substantial gap between multicultural education as applied in schools and the conditions of integration at school and work of children not belonging to majority cultural groups. In response to alarming situations (violent cultural conflicts, inequality, the development of ethnic ghettos in major cities) schools came up with educational solutions (bilingual education in the United States, the inclusion of ethnic courses in curricula, the creation of special classes). It is inappropriate to condemn schools for the relatively ineffective initiatives that they took, or for their indifference: the problem was not only poorly defined but also was not really one for them to resolve.

In these circumstances it is not surprising that multicultural education policies seem confused and ill–ordered. Churchill tried to put proposals and programmes into categories[3] while Verne[4] endeavoured to give proper perspective to the interactions between cultural and political movements, between education policies and school responses, and between the aspirations of minority ethnic groups and those of majority public opinion.

Two further key points in the conceptual framework of this report come from Verne's paper. The first is the importance of central government involvement in the organisation of inter–ethnic relations. The unusual point is not so much the interest which governments take in these problems, but rather the attitude of the ethnic communities. For years, most governments intervened in relations between different linguistic and cultural groups to promote and defend the interests of the dominant group. Even so, most under–privileged groups still continue to look to the State to satisfy their demands. This reaction can be interpreted in two ways: it can be considered contradictory, illogical and as a sign of weakness or it may be seen as indicating an improvement in the functioning of democracies as a result of pressure by civil rights and human rights movements. This trend has led several governments to adopt positions which are less hostile, less rigid and more neutral towards the aspirations of minority groups, and to amend the law to strengthen their cultural and linguistic rights.

The second key point that emerges from Verne's paper emphasizes the progressive institutionalisation of responses to economic and social problems in society, as though society had lost all self–regulatory capacity and now needed to live under constant supervision from the political authority. Official cognisance of the cultural and linguistic problems of minority ethnic groups, and the very fact that cultural and linguistic questions are treated as problems by official agencies, are a sign of the hold that official institutions have taken on present–day society. This trend can however be given the opposite interpretation. Government intervention might be seen as necessary to put right past injustices and to combat discrimination affecting minorities. Institutional machinery gradually set up following political victories by groups concerned with human rights does not then threaten individual freedom or in any way prevent social activities or voluntary work. On the contrary, the new legislation, by tackling concealed or established forms of discrimination against minority ethnic groups, opens up new prospects for development, as is shown by the results of the equal opportunities policy. Far from paralysing cultural and social life, official regulation lessens the most flagrant inequalities and encourages social and cultural activities, thanks to the greater opportunities and possibilities of social mobility given to members of minority groups. This calls to mind Lamennais who said that, as between the weak and the strong, liberty oppresses whereas the law liberates.

On the basis of this analysis, multicultural education is seen as the answer to the educational problems of children not belonging to the majority cultural groups. Other solutions could probably be considered but to do so one would have to go beyond the analytical framework in which government action has the prime place. From this standpoint, it might be concluded that multicultural education as currently offered in most countries is dominated by a certain form of analysis and political approach. However, from another standpoint this summary view might be disputed, since it can be shown that education systems are relatively independent of the political system[5]. This independence, forming a break in the close subordination of educational systems to government, is important since it allows for possible changes to structures and curricula which can lead, among other things, to multicultural education. By taking advantage of this, multicultural education, as it came into being and developed, would no longer be dominated by but would rather confirm the freedom and strength of the education system. Multicultural education programmes can then be devised with reference to some or all of the following aims:

— To combat the ethnocentricity of school culture and legitimate the presence in schools of other cultures;
— To educate children without putting them in a false position vis-à-vis their parents or their culture, i.e. by ensuring continuity between the school and the family;
— To present the teaching of languages and cultures as positive acquisitions rather than as imposed disciplines;
— To eliminate discrimination and prejudice in teaching;
— To bring about equal opportunities for everyone;
— To guarantee the pluralism of educational systems and schools;
— To respect the rights of children.

A study of the organisation, content, development and impact of multicultural education could have been designed on the lines of such programmes. However, the papers by Verne and Churchill, by showing the complexity of what underlies the organisation of multicultural education, raised more questions than they answered. These two writers, by revealing crucial unresolved questions at the scientific level, drew attention to the dangers of developing a facile and respectable type of multicultural education. This being so, it was necessary to look in detail at the underlying requirements of multicultural education and the preconditions for its implementation: before examining content, it was appropriate to consider form. Six points were considered in greater detail:

— Cultural and linguistic identity;
— The growing cultural uniformity of advanced industrial societies;
— Cultural relativism;
— The new minorities;
— Multilingual contexts;
— The ethnic dilemma.

Cultural identity

We have already noted that identity is a key concept in writings on multicultural education; it is one that is hard to employ in relation to communities, and even more so when dealing with the interaction between community identity and individual identity, as is the case in education. As a topic for exploration in social psychology, this is precarious ground.

Publications in English, especially from North America, increasingly use the concept of ethnicity rather than identity. What does this switch mean, why is it being made, and what approach does it reflect? Changes of terminology are not neutral in an area of this kind; they are even less neutral as we move from one language to another or from one culture to another. The same term — in this case identity or ethnicity — may take on different meanings. This aspect can be left to one side for the moment. What concerns us here is the shift taking place from one term to another one with different shades of meaning to refer to the same reality. This must be investigated since it concerns one of the most popular concepts in discussions about multicultural education.

The use of the term "ethnicity" to describe what was previously known as "cultural identity" shows that the term "identity" is no longer functioning properly. Morin[6] notes that "ethnicity" is a recent concept, first used in the United States in the 1950s to describe the reassertion of ethnic identity and demands for equal rights by minorities in education and at work. In passing from politics to science the concept of ethnicity changed to become a tool for the accurate description of minorities, the classification of ethnic groups and measurement of the gap between a community's view of itself and the way it is seen by the dominant society "from the outside". According to Raveau[7], to overcome the ambiguity of the expression "cultural identity" and to dissipate the confusion surrounding it (which is the source of increasing misunderstanding among those dealing with multiculturalism and multicultural education), an efficient tool of analysis has to be found to establish or identify empirically the objective differences between minority groups. Ethnicity, according to this writer, enables the construction of an objective ethnic profile using seven indicators, i.e. biogenetic, territorial, linguistic, economic, religious, cultural and political. Morin, in his commentary on the proposal by Raveau, queries the utility of this typology in the following terms: "Are we to establish a hierarchy of minorities? With high ethnicity or low ethnicity? Showing that some minorities are handicapped by their ethnicity which is "too visible" and so find it difficult to integrate?" Raveau does not reply to these questions but proposes that the host or dominant society also be measured for ethnicity in this way. Confrontation of these profiles should make it possible "to establish a dialogue and policies for education".

Greater cultural uniformity

In examining interactions between cultures, which are one of the key aspects of pluralism and multicultural education, Verne[8] drew attention to the apparently contradictory nature of the development of contemporary culture: on the one hand, there is the search for cultural authenticity, the return to origins, the need to preserve minor languages, pride in particularisms, admiration for cultural self–sufficiency and maintenance of traditions; on the other hand, we find the spread of a uniform world culture, the emergence of supranational myths and the adoption of similar lifestyles in widely differing settings. Modern technological societies have generated a transnational, composite, mass culture with its own language whose linguistic imprint is already universally evident.

Multicultural education programmes are bound to reflect this situation, i.e. confrontation between local, national and regional cultures (the geographical reference here is solely to underline the differences between traditional cultures) and confrontation of those cultures with the world culture which is increasingly coming to absorb them. In the best sense, multicultural education should involve comparing cultures. Such an exercise cannot be seriously undertaken in the absence of terms of reference and a working method. The former encompass the whole body of values, beliefs and knowledge which have come to form the cultural capital of a community; the method has to be the scientific method. The systematic study of other cultures, confrontation of varying opinions, doubt as to underlying assumptions is one of the

17

characteristics of the Western academic (and hence educational) tradition. Since the ancient Greeks (e.g. Herodotus giving his compatriots a public account of his travels in Persia) Western culture has continued to study other cultures, to discover similarities and differences, and to adopt anything of use in approaching truth and absolute good. We can speak in this connection of the universalist vocation of the school, and of the culture of the school. This universalism obviously has little in common with that of the cathodic matrix of the new world culture. The universalism of educational culture is that of rational thought: it proceeds by establishing distinctions, differences and hierarchies through the ordering of knowledge in the constant search for truth. It is thus quite unlike the univeralism of a cultural relativism which dilutes beliefs and values and blurs differences.

The position of multicultural education seems ambiguous here, caught between hammer and anvil: on one side, the educational tradition of critical and rationalist thinking, on the other, the struggle against explicit and concealed forms of ethnocentrism (the source of a great deal of discrimination against minorities) and acceptance of pluralism. Multicultural education programmes which do not take account of this contradiction, and do not take a firm stand at the cognitive level, are likely to end in second–rate folklore or run counter to the aim of equal opportunities.

Cultural relativism

Education in State schools has an emancipating function: by teaching how to read and write, i.e. by divulging written culture, school constitutes a radical break in the way knowledge is transmitted and opens up unlimited possibilities for cultural enrichment[9]. In societies with writing, knowledge is derived from books rather than simply from circumstances, as is the case in oral societies. Education emancipates in cognitive terms since it makes possible the transmission and acquisition of knowledge regardless of local circumstances. This explains the continual tension in relations between school and the family, as an emblematic institution for the contextual transmission of knowledge, and between school and local communities which still aspire to control teaching in schools. What is the place of multicultural education in the State schools of the democratic societies? This question implies discussing the relations between the univeralism of the scholastic tradition and the specificities of ethnic traditions to be found within modern pluralist societies. Implementation of multicultural education programmes in the present–day education systems of the OECD Member countries is not as simple and straightforward as is sometimes thought. In no case is it merely a question of good or bad faith. What is the meaning of opening schools to other cultures, adapting curricula in a multicultural direction? Musgrove[10] has examined the influence on Western educational organisation of a number of scientists who in certain disciplines (notably cultural anthropology, psychology, sociology) have studied the interactions between cultures and opened the way to relativist theories which have exerted considerable influence on the multicultural education movement. Since in the education systems of the OECD Member countries school is the place where children go to learn and to acquire the mental skills specific to rational thought, it is essential, before implementing a multicultural education programme, to enquire into the epistemological structures of ways of thinking and forms of knowledge specific to different cultural traditions. The problem is not only that of the equivalence of cultures (cultural relativism) but also that of their epistemological equivalence

18

(epistemological relativism). The development of multicultural education requires the clearer definition and perception of the meaning of the rational thought and scientific knowledge which has hitherto constituted the basis of education in the OECD countries.

Another aspect of this question has been expounded by de Certeau[11] who queried the meaning of the presence, within highly educated societies patterned on the rationalist culture of the Enlightenment, of fragments, traces and survivals of ancestral cultures with different cognitive paradigms. In his analysis de Certeau showed that it would be fallacious to state the problem of values in an exclusive or radical form, postulating the integration or exclusion of alternative modes of life. Present–day societies can survive and operate only if different cultures can coexist, and individuals, depending on circumstances and needs, can move from one culture to another and experience several cultures. In the light of this consideration, the multicultural education programme acquires an entirely new scope and depth since its *raison d'être* is no longer based solely on ethical arguments (to fight discrimination due to racism or ethnocentrism) or legal arguments (respect for human rights) but also on epistemological arguments (differences in ways of thinking, forms of understanding and in the structure of knowledge). This enrichment of the conceptual framework suggests that it may be possible to construct a scientific theory of multicultural education and thus develop scientifically based multicultural education programmes.

The new minorities

In the past we had education policies for minorities rather than policies for multicultural education. Over recent decades there has been a gradual shift: education policies for minorities have been abandoned and their place has been taken by multicultural education policies. The process is significant in several ways. It indicates the emergence of a new way of looking at the question, it reflects a new awareness and a changed view of a given set of circumstances, without those circumstances necessarily having changed themselves — a new vision does not mean that the educational conditions facing minorities have radically (or even partly) altered.

The concept of multicultural education is moreover vague and imprecise. Are we dealing with education programmes directed solely at children in ethnic groups made up largely of immigrants and living among the rest of the school population (being mixed in proportions that vary substantially from one school to another), or new educational programmes developed in the framework of the traditional policies concerning conventional territorial minorities? Churchill[12], to classify these programmes, opted for a broad approach and put education programmes for immigrants' children, aborigines and minority ethnic groups all together.

Is it possible to argue, however, that there is little or no difference between immigrants and conventional minorities? For instance, is it possible to put Algerians and Bretons on the same footing in France, as de Certeau somewhat provocatively suggests[13]? Can migrant groups be regarded as minorities? They are minority groups, of course, but is it sufficient for them to be treated as minorities? This embarrassing question arises because what is at issue, behind the substitution of one term for another (minority instead of immigrant) is the linkage between the political and cultural spheres. The distinctions between ethnic communities are no longer the same and acquire a new meaning outside the legal framework. Distinctions that seemed obvious and accepted now appear less clearcut. New alliances and possibilities for action emerge on the basis of common interests which break down barriers between minority groups and put an end to their isolation in geographical and legal terms, thus making intercommunity contacts possible, contacts which constitute one of the constituent elements of a multicultural education programme.

Multilingual contexts

Language teaching occupies a central position in multicultural education, and the organisation of minority language classes is one of the main themes in discussions. In education circles there is a tendency to consider teaching a language (i.e. the inclusion in curricula of lessons in a language other than the designated language of instruction) to be essential to safeguard that language. The movement advocating the teaching of languages of origin or heritage languages is not based solely on linguistic considerations. Another argument, ethical or political in nature, is used to support it: this maintains that education in the mother tongue is an inalienable human right.

Then there are educational considerations: the use at school of languages spoken in the home would help bring about equal opportunity and would make education more effective, as a series of experiments in various countries tend to prove. This does not however mean that any form of bilingual instruction or language teaching programme will produce this result. Such conclusion would not be borne out by research. To obtain good results certain conditions must be met. Identification of the relevant parameters is one of the most promising fields of enquiry, as shown by the work of Cummins[14] on bilingual education. Neither should we neglect the fact that the development of bilingual education and language teaching programmes helps improve educational efficiency. In contemporary pluralist societies a knowledge of several languages is a considerable advantage both for the individual and for society. With regard to the close interdependence of national economies and the importance of world trade in the growth of modern economies, it is essential to promote knowledge of foreign languages, of minority languages[15] and even of less well–known languages. An education system which was unable to make the best use of children's linguistic knowledge, failed to encourage languages spoken in the home, and did not favour the survival of the country's minority languages would be less effective from any point of view. However, it must be stressed that this conclusion should not be seen as indiscriminately giving the go–ahead to all programmes for teaching languages and cultures of origin. The validity of the principle should not be confused with the validity of the solutions adopted. A great deal of work remains to be done here since in most countries the gap between the conclusions reached by research and practice remains considerable.

Science must and can examine the effectiveness of bilingual or multilingual education and produce a sound theory of multicultural education with satisfactory predictive value. The decision to implement bilingual or multilingual education programmes is however a matter for the political authorities. The status of languages in education is largely a political issue, and is closely dependent on the directions of linguistic policy, national priorities concerning language, and the degree of availability or openness of society to linguistic differences. The paper by Bratt Paulston on linguistic policies[16] clearly brings out the imbrication of divergant and sometimes conflictual interests and motivations underlying any linguistic policy.

The ethnic dilemma

What benefit accrues to minority ethnic groups from the introduction of ethnic courses, minority languages and multicultural education into school curricula? Over and above the symbolic aspect of programmes of this kind, whose inclusion in curricula is usually understood as a gesture of respect, recognition and confidence by the culturally dominant group towards minorities (evidence, by the way, of the school's force as a forum for cultural legitimation), what is their real impact on educational performance and equality of opportunity? What are their benefits for children from minority ethnic groups? Do the adoption of an intercultural approach in education and the introduction of multicultural or native language and culture lessons reduce the high rates of under-achievement found among these children?

These questions concern the compatibility of two postulates of education policies, i.e. equality and respect for differences. The difficulties encountered with equal-opportunity policies and recent discussions on the quality of education show that no satisfactory solution has yet been found. The problem is even more complex in the case of children from minority ethnic groups. Since the results obtained so far have not always been convincing, doubt is beginning to be expressed in certain circles as to the suitability of specific action to improve the situation. This reaction is excessive; the poor results indicate that the solutions proposed are perhaps inadequate, but do not justify the assertion that there are no possible solutions.

The recognition of cultural differences by education systems has proved to be two-edged: it may penalise children in ethnic groups as individuals when, in the name of a policy to protect or recognise the rights of minorities or ethnic communities, their liberty of choice is restricted by compelling them (through pressure, continual insistence, and one-sided advice) to follow courses designed exclusively for them, to study certain subjects rather than others, and to seek out custom-made curricula implemented in agreement with the ethnic communities or national education authorities. In this case, children to some extent become hostages tied to a particular culture as a result of their ethnic origin. This is what happens when individual identity is confused with collective identity.

It could also be maintained that the ethnic dilemma is a false problem since it only arises when multicultural programmes addressed specifically at minorities are introduced. If multicultural programmes were prepared for the majority (which would in itself be highly logical) or if they covered all children without distinction, there would be no ethnic dilemma. Unfortunately, in practice, it is rather the opposite that occurs. With some exceptions multicultural education programmes are usually aimed at children in ethnic groups. There is therefore indeed an ethnic dilemma. There has to be awareness of this and minorities have to be alerted to the consequences of all short and medium-term decisions. It cannot be denied that certain options are likely to have serious consequences both for children's development as individuals and for the political future of minorities.

NOTES AND REFERENCES

1. Churchill, S.: *The Education of Linguistic and Cultural Minorities in the OECD Countries.* Multilingual Matters Ltd., Clevedon, 1986.
2. Specific contributions to the ECALP project were received from Australia, Finland, Greece, Italy, Luxembourg, New Zealand, Portugal, Spain and Yugoslavia. A number of countries, including Canada, the Netherlands and Sweden, provided considerable material but did not submit an official report.
3. Churchill, S.: *op. cit.*
4. Verne, E.: "Multicultural education policies: a critical analysis". In *Multicultural Education*, OECD/CERI, Paris, 1987.
5. Archer, S.M.: *The Sociology of Educational Expansion. Take-off, Growth and Inflation in Educational Systems.* Sage, London, 1982.
6. Morin, F.: "Commentary on Raveau's paper: Ethnicity, Migrations and Minorities". In *Multicultural Education*, OECD/CERI, *op. cit.*
7. Raveau, F.H.M.: "Ethnicity, Migrations and Minorities". In *Multicultural Education*, OECD/CERI, *op. cit.*
8. Verne, E.: *op. cit.*
9. Literacy constitutes a revolution of communications techniques with immense consequences, carefully documented in the research by Goody (see J. Goody: *The domestication of the savage mind*, Cambridge University Press, Cambridge, 1977 and by the same author, *La logique de l'écriture. Aux origines des sociétés humaines*, Colin, Paris, 1986).
10. We may simply refer here to Musgrove, F.: *Education and Anthropology. Other Cultures and the Teacher*, John Wiley & Sons, Chichester, 1982, which makes a full presentation of the problem of cultural relativism in education and provides an extensive survey of the bibliography.
11. De Certeau, M.: "The management of ethnic resources: Schooling for diversity". In *Multicultural Education*, OECD/CERI, *op. cit.*
12. Churchill, S.: *op. cit.*
13. De Certeau, M.: *op. cit.*
14. Cummins, J.: "Theory and Policy in Bilingual Education". In *Multicultural Education*, OECD/CERI, *op. cit.*
15. The term "minority language" must be understood in the relative sense, bearing in mind the position in a given country. Spanish is a minority language in the United States, for instance, but not of course in Mexico.
16. Bratt Paulston, C.: "Linguistic Consequences of Ethnicity and Nationalism in Multilingual Settings". In *Multicultural Education*, OECD/CERI, *op. cit.*

Chapter II

THE MULTICULTURAL CONTEXT

The multicultural or pluriethnic trend apparent in most OECD countries is clearly affecting education and is creating numerous problems for teachers and those in charge of education. This multicultural reality is to be found everywhere: it is seen in the changes in the ethnic make–up of towns and cities, but is also perceptible in social behaviour and attitudes. This visible and yet intangible reality shapes the frame of reference for multicultural education policies.

The socio–geographical context

One single society in the OECD area, Iceland, is culturally homogeneous: the nation is identified with the State, and both are identified with the country. That is the exception. Everywhere else we find situations with cultural and ethnic admixtures of varying sorts and degrees, and a co–existence of differences: races, ethnic groups and nationalities, not to mention cultures and languages, are intermingled, superimposed, wax and wane, merge or move, and sometimes preserve real or imagined ties with a point of origin, a homeland, or elsewhere. There is no country that is entirely free from multiculturalism. Cultural diversity is the rule, as is ethnic pluralism.

The strains and constrasts, conflicts and syntheses generated by these encounters are essential for the vitality of democracy and fruitful for the cultural enrichment of the societies that accept them. The vigour of the countries of the American continent, and of Australia and New Zealand, demonstrates the validity of this observation. The diversity of peoples and nations within a State is not however an exclusive characteristic of these countries; the main European countries have always been assemblies of minorities[1]. This situation has everywhere and at all times led to policies of unification, and of forced marginalisation and acculturation or assimilation of minorities. These policies are simply the reflection of multiculturalism in society and have developed throughout modern history, going hand in hand with the birth and development of modern States[2]. The political model of one State, one language, one culture and indeed one religion, which took over with the emergence of the Nation State, made them indispensable[3]. From the standpoint of the Nation State, the presence of minorities is a problem[4] worsened by the cultural and ethnic changes flowing from the large–scale movements of people after the splintering of major empires, mass emigration for economic reasons, and political persecution.

While these factors have increased in scale during the present era, it must be remembered that the presence of minorities, and indeed the development of emigration, are not in themselves the problem, because neither is new. Difficulties relate to the conception of the role and functioning of the State and to the reactions of society to cultural pluralism. It is likely that the multicultural issue will remain a difficult one until such time as there is a change in political thinking and in the criteria of unity and uniformity which underlie the workings of government.

The scale of the demographic and socio–cultural changes of recent decades explains why the ethnic question has become so acute in political terms in all the OECD countries. A few examples will illustrate why this is so.

One significant case is *Sweden*. Although it had two historic minorities in the north (Lapps and Finns), until 1930 the country was ethnically homogenous: a single language, a single race, a single religion. One minister handling the immigration portfolio described his country as having a culturally egocentric frame of mind, by no means ready to accept immigrants' cultures and languages[5]. For 80 years Sweden had a clear migration deficit: between 1851 and 1930 1.5 million Swedes emigrated, chiefly to the United States[6]. The outward flow began to reverse after the 1929 slump, which led to a substantial number of Swedish Americans returning. The number of immigrants has risen steadily since then, giving rise to one of the most significant social changes in all Sweden's history[7], and has made Sweden the most ethnically differentiated Scandinavian country: today, out of eight million people, one million are of non–Swedish origin[8].

Another Nordic country, *Denmark*, unlike Sweden, long remained outside the mainstream of migration. The small German minority in Schleswig, in the South, posed no threat to the country's cultural homogeneity. This almost idyllic picture is now affected by the sudden arrival of foreign migrants and political refugees who are introducing new languages and cultures into Denmark. Though located essentially in the Copenhagen area, this development surprised and disturbed the authorities and public opinion. In 1975 there were 2 092 foreign children at school in Denmark. Eight years later the figure had risen almost fivefold, to stand at 9 825 in November 1983. To gauge the scale of the inflow we need to consider, alongside the children, their parents and other family members, and the adults with no children. Furthermore, the Danish authorities have for some years been coping with a traditional–type majority–minority confrontation, i.e. relations with the autonomous governments of the Faroe Islands and Greenland where lesser used languages are spoken. But this issue has now been separated (or was until recently) from the new problem.

A neighbouring country, *Germany*, long remained closed to foreign penetration. Until relatively recently it was monolingual. That altered in 1955, the date of the first immigration agreement with Italy, and changes came very quickly with the enormous flow of labour following the closure of the border with the German Democratic Republic in 1961. Other agreements on immigration were signed with Greece and Spain in 1960, Turkey in 1961, Morocco in 1963, Portugal in 1964, Tunisia in 1965 and Yugoslavia in 1968. That enumeration itself speaks of the demand for manpower in the rapidly expanding German economy. At the outset of the period there were no more than 80 000 migrant workers in Germany (0.3 per cent of the labour force). Ten years later the figure had doubled, and peaked in 1975 with 2 million foreign workers, representing a little under 10 per cent of the labour force. In thirty years, between 1955 and 1985, the foreign population in Germany rose from a few hundred thousand (686 000 in June 1961) to over 4 million — a massive shock for a country with no experience of cultural and linguistic change on such a scale. The growth of Turkish immigration illustrates this cultural explosion: in 1970 Turkish nationals numbered about 500 000 in Germany, roughly level with Italians and Yugoslavs. Their numbers have tripled since then and stood at 1.5 million in 1982, making the Turks the largest of all the foreign communities established in Germany. According to projections by the Federal Ministry for Labour and Social Affairs, the foreign population is expected to reach 6 million in 1990 and 7 million in the year 2000, posing problems of integration on such a scale that they will be difficult to handle if appropriate measures are not taken in the meantime[9].

It is easy enough to see why this swift and unexpected development has shocked and surprised countries which had been relatively sheltered, until recent times, from any cultural admixture. It is harder to understand why the reaction should have been the same in countries which have historically been meeting grounds for different cultures and civilisations. Perhaps the most curious case in this respect is the *United Kingdom*, where the demographic picture is much the same. In 1951 apparently no more than 75 000 people or 0.2 per cent of the population — almost insignificant in statistical terms — belonged to racial minorities. By 1974 the figure had risen to 1.6 million, or roughly 3 per cent of the population. In a quarter of a century the United Kingdom had undergone a very significant cultural and linguistic transformation. As a result of this rapid change the British education system suddenly found itself faced, after 1960, with the multicultural problem. In 1972 the coloured classroom population was put at 279 872, almost 4 per cent of the total enrolment, whereas it had been practically non–existent in 1960.

As a final example from Europe we may look at *France*. As well as having several regional minorities, the country has over the centuries received a large number of different ethnic groups — to the extent that some writers[10] have argued that the high degree of centralisation in French government machinery was the unavoidable counterpart of the cultural and linguistic mosaic: in the absence of a strong central authority the country might have splintered at any moment. The immigration of 15–20 million workers between 1851 and 1975 merely heightened the complex socio–cultural interactions. In the inter–war period France ranked with the United States as one of the main countries for immigration. Between 1921 and 1926 the foreign population rose by 66 per cent. Migratory flows slackened after the 1931 crisis and migration did not resume apace again until 1955. Over a million people settled in France between 1968 and 1973. This was the second major wave of migration this century, changing the social landscape radically and upsetting balances that had been painfully achieved. The present situation is not comparable to that at the start of the century, admittedly, but the similarity of reactions may indicate that the French–style melting pot will, over the medium and long term, prevail again.

That leads us naturally to the melting pot of the United States, and other countries which have been formed through immigration and are a cultural mosaic as a result. In the *United States* current statistics acknowledge four major minority groups: American Indians, whose number rose from 800 000 in 1970 to 1.4 million in 1980, a 75 per cent increase over ten years; Blacks, certainly the largest minority, representing

12 per cent of the population (more or less 25 million at the beginning of the 1980s); Hispanics, with a 60 per cent increase between 1970 and 1980, rising from 9.1 to 14.6 million to represent 6.4 per cent of the population; and Asians, whose numbers have doubled in ten years and stood at 3.5 million in 1980. These expanding groups pose the most acute education problems in terms of equality of opportunity.

In *Australia* in 1978 77 per cent of the population was descended from the initial Anglo–Celtic group; the remainder, leaving aside the Aborigines[11], was distributed over more than a hundred linguistic groups[12]. Very few OECD countries can show a comparable ethnic explosion; at the end of the Second World War Australia could still be regarded as a monolingual country. At present 40 per cent of the Australian population of 15 million is made up of first–generation migrants and their children. Half of these 6 million new Australians come from non–English–speaking countries with different cultural and linguistic traditions from the majority Anglo–Saxon group[13].

The urban changes

These data are impressive for their size, but give little idea of what is happening on the ground, for minorities are not distributed uniformly. Every country has some regions which have remained untouched and other regions, especially major urban centres and suburbs, where there are high concentrations of different ethnic groups.

To grasp the scale and in some cases the dramatic nature of this ethnic mix we need to consider the changes that have taken place in metropolitan populations.

In Europe this development is found not only in the major cosmopolitan capitals, such as Paris and London, but in medium–sized cities as well. *Cologne*, in Germany, is an example: with 147 000 foreigners in a population of a million, it ranks fourth in Germany for foreigners in total population (14.4 per cent), after Frankfurt, Stuttgart and Munich. The first foreign workers arrived in the city in the 1960s. In 1961 there were 11 000, mostly Italians (7 133); there were only 124 Turks at that time. In the later 1960s local industry began recruiting Turkish workers in large numbers. The total rose, between 1961 and 1970, from 124 to 22 147; by 1975 there was a Turkish community of 42 450, and 66 000 by 1981, making this the largest group, ahead of Italians (23 718), Yugoslavs (9 200) and Greeks (7 700).

This population lives in 18 of the 83 districts of Cologne. In the city centre 33 per cent of the population is of foreign origin; in all the industrial areas the figure ranges between a low of 20.8 per cent (Nichl) and a high of 28.2 per cent (Kalk). In several areas the small retail and restaurant trade is in foreign hands[14].

Bradford, in the United Kingdom, presents a similar picture. Towards the end of the 1950s the local textile industry began recruiting workers from Kashmir, Mirpur and Pakistan. A short time later these men brought their wives and children over and in the early 1960s the first Asian children began attending local schools. To avoid concentrations, the local education authorities decided that pupils from ethnic groups should not exceed 10 per cent in any school and to maintain this level Asian children were bussed within Bradford. The system operated until 1979, when the threshold had risen to 33 per cent. In 1981 one in ten of the city's population had been born outside the United Kingdom, an eloquent indicator of the social transformation that occurred over the last 20 years. By 1984 one child in five used a language other than English at home: 62 per cent spoke Punjabi, 15 per cent Urdu, 8 per cent Gujerati and 5 per cent Bengali. The forecasts for the coming 20 years are still more significant. The local authorities expect that the black population (the term used to cover the population of Indian, Pakistani, Bangladeshi and West Indian origin) will increase by 29 000 over the next 20 years, and rise from 62 000 in 1984 to 91 000 in 1996[15].

A similar trend is found in *Glasgow*, again not in a central position. In 1979 3 595 children in the city's schools were not of English mother tongue; just three years later, in 1982, the figure was 4 481, or an increase of some 25 per cent[16].

Major cities outside Europe have not been exempt from these cultural tremors either. There have been spectacular changes everywhere. In *Toronto*, towards the mid–1970s, over half of the school population was of non–English–speaking origin. In *Los Angeles* in 1960 one person in nine was of Hispanic origin and one in a hundred Asian; a quarter of a century later Hispanics represented a third of the city's population, and Asians one–tenth. There is no longer an ethnic majority in Los Angeles: everyone belongs to one minority or another, including the Anglo–Saxons[17]. That is certainly an extreme situation, but are Sydney, Montreal, New York, London or Paris very different? Multiculturalism is a fact of life in all these major cities, which have become multiethnic, polyglot centres where, culturally at least, there is no longer any clearly defined majority or minority.

The terminological misunderstandings

This changing multicultural landscape is as hard to define as a kaleidoscope: most of the conceptual categories employed in discussion and analysis are ambiguous and do not help us to advance. The words do not identify and define a mobile reality where distinctions constantly vary and merge. The vagueness of the concepts, as Sayad notes[18], is the prime reason for the fashion of using certain terms that mean both everything and nothing, which are apparently easy for everyone to understand because they are vague and imprecise[19]. We think we all understand the same thing, but the reverse is actually the case, on account of the numerous interpretations that the terms can have[20].

This state of affairs, which has permeated the area of education, is not disappearing. The manifold meanings applied to words are in fact increasing so that it is sometimes hard to draw any distinction between multicultural education, intercultural education and bilingual education.

The increasing number of terms with similar meanings marks the emergence of fresh representations of the multicultural situation without there being any real changes in relations between minority and majority ethnic groups[21].

Throughout all the discussions about multicultural education we continually come up against the same difficulty — that of finding appropriate terminology to address the subject at the international level. The usual terms, heavily laden with historical and political connotations, stand in the way of precise analysis which can grasp and express tensions and shades of meaning in the perception of problems. Sayad lucidly outlined the difficulties of interpreting the term *minority*:

"Minority" logically contrasts with "majority", as "dominated" contrasts with "dominant". But if the expression is not to be an absolute, an abstraction, or an attribute detached from the conditions in which it is effectively applied, it would be better to specify on each occasion in what respect a minority position is being referred to. To be in a "minority" absolutely (i.e. in all relationships and all fields of existence) would ultimately mean no longer to exist or no longer to exist independently — to depend for one's existence on others. It would also involve receiving and accepting (with no alternative) the designation "minority" as given and imposed by others — to be defined by others (hetero–definition instead of self–definition) as being in a "minority". Conversely, to define oneself willingly as being in a "minority" ... is to affirm one's existence as such, proclaim one's independence and guard against any identification with the others. It is to choose the criterion by which one regards oneself as in a "minority". Those two ways of being in a "minority" are clearly poles apart, contradictory in all points. The populations they concern are different. So are the historical backgrounds leading up to the formation of the two kinds of "minority" position, the relationships with respect to those positions and the ways of conforming to them, i.e. of behaving (the ways of assuming the "minority" condition and the ways of behaving in that condition)"[22].

Confusion also surrounds the expression *linguistic minority*, a term common in writings about multicultural education. At first sight a definition does not seem to pose any special difficulty: a linguistic minority will apparently be a group of people speaking a language other than the one spoken by the majority of the population in a given country[23], or people who have in common a language that is not the dominant language[24], such as Hispanics in the United States, West Indians in Britain, or Arabic speakers in France. Yet this apparently simple explanation raises a number of questions regarding levels of knowledge of the minority language, formalisation, individual and collective use. The solutions adopted distinguish one linguistic minority from another, so that they cannot all be put on the same footing or treated in the same way[25]. It is still more difficult to determine membership; relations with a language are essentially subjective and symbolic, and there are no adequate indicators to identify objective membership of a linguistic minority, for in this area language use is less relevant than the affective or sentimental tie that may exist[26]. Accordingly, membership of a linguistic minority cannot be either proven or laid down by bureaucratic means[27]. That is the main stumbling block in all language research.

Another ambiguous term, used in a variety of different ways, is *multiculturalism* which covers a current of ideas, an ideology or a set of cultural circumstances (e.g. the multiculturalism of society "x"). The concept is vague as regards the interaction of neighbouring cultures: it may indicate osmosis, exchange, or mixture of cultures or simply juxtaposition. It is also used to refer to the impact on minority cultures when they come into contact with the dominant culture, which is often taken to be the majority culture. In that sense the dominant culture falls outside the sphere of multiculturalism, so we have on the one side the groups which are the object of multicultural policies (ethnic minorities, migrants, aborigines, linguistic minorities) and on the other the majority group which makes that policy for the rest (for those who are different) and is not itself affected by multiculturalism. The semantic shift from a sense that embraces all the groups to an exclusive sense that covers only certain groups, often leaving out just the majority group, is common[28]. The term lends itself admirably to this open and yet closed stance, both recognising and negating pluralism[29].

Looking specifically at education, we find the same proliferation of meanings around multicultural and intercultural education. The vagueness surrounding *multicultural education* conceals two opposing approaches: one which regards multicultural education as a new teaching discipline to be included in the curriculum, and one which sees it as a general approach, a state of mind which must permeate the whole curriculum. In the first there is a formalist interpretation of multicultural education, as an activity in the school timetable, taking place at given periods, and studied as a sphere of knowledge. Children do multicultural education as they do maths or civics. In the second approach the interpretation is an informal one: multicultural education is a routine practice, and covers a state of mind, conduct and collective lifestyle that is developed at school[30]. Multicultural education thus ends up, in the second case, by becoming identified with plain education: learning tolerance and a critical attitude would in itself be multicultural education. We thus move from a limited conception of multicultural education, when the term refers to courses on cultural and linguistic diversity, with a vaguely ethnological connotation, to a broader, diffuse conception that identifies multicultural education with social and civic education. Multicultural education would then involve wider issues than those relating to the cohabitation of different cultures. It would, for example, include the problems of racism, sexism and participation in social and political life. Despite this ambiguity[31], the term has gained popularity and is in extensive use. It is also used in this report for it is a convenient term, but it should be noted that CERI has avoided using it for a project dealing with a broader sphere, the development of education when confronted by cultural and linguistic pluralism.

The picture is no clearer in attempting to define *interculturalism* and intercultural education. This is another educational nebula of the first magnitude. The term's meanings are once again vague, an area for consideration and discussion[32]. Interculturalism is so difficult to define that it is generally presented as a state of mind, a question of attitudes[33]: interculturalism is apparently a militant virtue[34], practised by missionaries who believe in a new society built upon brotherhood, love and understanding among mankind. We can perceive, in a shadowy way, a concern to avoid the perils of the splintering of the social structure, the rupture that may come from any attempt at secession, or the equal perils of minorities splintering, and disappearing through assimilation. According to Micheline Rey Von Allmen, who for a considerable period was rapporteur for the Council of Europe project concerned with intercultural education, from this standpoint "it is not a matter either of forcing migrants — children or adults — to wear their origin on their sleeve and to identify themselves with their country's culture, or of assimilating them against their wishes into the society of the receiving country, but of offering them the means to express their own individual or collective personality, to make their own cultural demands, as well as of seeing that they have the co-operation of the receiving country and of their own country in their effort to achieve an identity, freedom and fulfilment"[35]. The ambiguity found with multicultural education is also found in the intercultural sphere: it is interpreted either as a set of ethnic activities, reserved for migrant children or cultural minorities, or as a special course of teaching, addressed solely to children different from their fellows by reason of their passport, colour of their skin or language spoken outside school, or else as a general philosophy of education which imbues the whole of the curriculum. Porcher, one of the main analysts on intercultural education asserts that "if the intercultural policy is to be consistent and really effective it must be adopted generally and for everyone"; "an original type of education should be worked out, for the children of migrant workers specifically but including them necessarily among the target school population"; "it must be offered to all children"[36].

In spite of these similarities with multiculturalism, interculturalism differs somewhat in interpretation: it is both more axiomatic — dialogue between cultures is possible, greater openness to different cultures is in principle the best perspective, in political, moral and educational terms[37] — and more ideological, for it takes its stance on the ethics of conviction. Interculturalism is seen as a project, a hope, a hypothesis, a perspective, a long–term task to be unceasingly worked over, an ethical commitment, an ideal[38]. It is presented as going further than multiculturalism, transcending mere coexistence of different cultures, though without advocating that they should all be mixed in a single melting pot in order to forge a new social contract[39].

Finally, we consider the concepts of *bilingualism* and *bilingual education*, of which there are numerous variants[40]. It is necessary to distinguish between bilingualism as a linguistic phenomenon and bilingualism as a cultural and political phenomenon. In the latter case the term refers to a current of opinion which advocates the spread of bilingualism in society and hence implementation of a certain form of language policy. In linguistic terms individual bilingualism has to be distinguished from social or community bilingualism. We shall take a broad definition. Bilingualism is the knowledge and use of two languages by a single person, independent of the level of knowledge and intensity of use of each. Education in which instruction is given in two languages is hence termed bilingual. Bilingual education programmes address bilingual children or children who are becoming bilingual. The first and second languages are normally distinguished (L1 and L2). Here again, we find apparent clarity in principle: the first language (L1) should be the one the child learns first; usually it is identified with the language spoken at home. It is not necessarily the mother tongue[41]. In cases of diglossia or in polyglot communities, L1 is not easy to determine. The other language (L2) is the one learnt later; in some cases it is the language of schooling or of the country of settlement. In a few cases bilingual education continues throughout schooling; in Slovenia and Catalonia efforts are being made to apply a solution of this kind, whereas in Grisons Canton in Switzerland bilingual classes cover only part of the period of compulsory schooling. Bilingual education is often transitory; it ends with L1 being relinquished when L2 has been properly learnt or when the child can receive instruction in L2 without difficulty.

The imprecision of terms is no help to analysis or discussion. We have chosen here not to join the battle about the definitions. The words are taken in their broadest sense: that will not hamper our review, for the aim is not to draw a detailed chart of multicultural education where each individual area is clearly marked out, but to identify the issues and forces that underlie policies concerning multicultural education.

NOTES AND REFERENCES

1. Allardt, E.: "Ethnic Mobilisation and Minority Resources". Paper for the Colloquium on Understanding Political Society, held by the Werner–Reimers Stiftung in Bad Hamburg, 18th–22nd May 1981. Forty-six minorities are identified in all the European OECD countries but the list is incomplete because it includes only territorial minorities and does not take into account minorities that have appeared in recent decades (the Moluccans and Surinamese in the Netherlands, for example, or the West Indians and Pakistanis in the United Kingdom), and because a number of historic minorities have not been noted. The numerous Yugoslav minorities are not shown either. In the absence of an exact figure, it may hence be concluded that the number of minorities in the European area of the OECD is well over 50.

2. One of the first instances of intolerance towards minorities in the name of *raison d'Etat* was the systematic persecution of the Huguenots in France throughout the 17th Century, leading in 1685 to the Revocation of the Edict of Nantes by Louis XIV. A further stage in this process of unification was the decision under the Revolution, a century later, to prohibit the use of languages other than French in any official document. After a single religion and form of worship comes a single language. In this connection, see in particular de Certeau, M., Julia, D., Revel, J.: *Une politique de la langue. La Révolution française et les patois*, Gallimard, Paris, 1975.

3. The most striking example is the break-up of the multinational Austrian Empire. On the crisis in the Nation State system and the problems of managing minorities, see Arendt, H.: *The Origins of Totalitarianism*, 1951. According to Arendt, the internal disintegration of Nation States began only after the First World War, with the demands of those minorities which did not get their own Nation State under the Paris Treaties.

4. The difficulties in adopting the Nation State model in areas where minority population is dense is clear in the Yugoslav system, where the terminology distinguishes between the nations making up the State, nationalities, national minorities and minority ethnic groups. With this classification, a politico-administrative system had to be devised to enable them all to coexist in a single state entity.

5. Widgren, J.: "La xénophobie et les enfants. L'expérience suédoise", in *FORUM*, Council of Europe, Strasbourg, No. 1, 1984.

6. To give an idea of the scale of this movement, it should be noted that over a quarter of Sweden's population had then left. This emigration gave rise to one of the most impressive migratory flows of the past century. For further information, see Opper, S.: "Multiculturalism in Sweden: A case of assimilation and integration", in *Comparative Education*, Vol. 19, No. 2, 1983.

7. Bergman, E.: "A Swedish Dilemma. Ethnic Conflicts in Sweden", in *Current Sweden*, The Swedish Institute, Stockholm, No. 297, 1982.

8. The demographic impact of this influx of migrants and political refugees has been surprising too. The Swedish statistical office has estimated that without this wave of immigration, the population would have fallen by 780 000 between 1944 and 1976. Immigration contributed 46 per cent to population growth over that period ("Stateus om Invandrarverk", 1980, p. 9).

9. Bundesminister für Arbeit und Sozialordnung: *Sozialbericht 1983*, Bonn, 1984.

10. Le Bras, H., Todd, E.: *L'invention de la France*, Editions de Poche, Hachette, Paris, 1981.

11. It should be noted that Aborigines are not a homogeneous group and cannot be reduced to a single people. Indigenous society was multicultural and multilingual before the Europeans landed (approximately 250 languages were in use). The simplified, homogeneous picture of Aborigines

is a counterpart of the similar picture which the white Anglo-Saxon dominated society had of itself. After 200 years of European rule, "at least 50 Aboriginal languages are now extinct and another 100 face imminent death... Only 50 languages are in relatively healthy state, surviving against great odds for many years" (Parliament of the Commonwealth of Australia, Senate Standing Committee on Education and Arts, 1984, para. 8.7).

12. Mills, J.: "Bilingual Education in Australian Schools. A Review". Australian Council for Educational Research, 1982.

13. The vitality of the cultures found in Australia is apparent in the development of the non-English press, with over 100 titles in some 30 different languages, five daily newspapers, mostly in Italian and Greek, and weekly papers in many other languages.

14. Guezengar, A.: "Immigration et petits commerces étrangers dans la ville de Cologne (RFA)", in *Marchands ambulants et commerçants étrangers en France et en Allemagne fédérale*, Centre Interuniversitaire d'Etudes Méditerranéennes, Université de Poitiers, Fascicule 7, 1984.

15. Bradford Metropolitan Council, 1984.

16. Grant, C.A.: "Multicultural Teacher Education — Renewing the Discussion: A Response to Martin Haberman", in *Journal of Teacher Education*, Vol. XXXIV, No. 2, 1983.

17. Under the title "Ethnic Explosion", *Time Magazine* (No. 24, 1983, p. 14) published a table of population figures for Los Angeles:

	1983	1970
Mexicans	2 100 000	822 300
Iranians	200 000	20 000
Salvadorans	200 000	fewer than 2 000
Japanese	175 000	104 000
Armenians	175 000	75 000
Chinese	153 000	41 000
Koreans	150 000	8 900
Filipinos	150 000	33 500
Israelis	90 000	10 000
Arab Americans	130 000	45 000
Guatemalans	50 000	fewer than 2 000
Vietnamese	40 000	fewer than 2 000

18. Sayad, A.: "From 'immigrants' to 'minorities' — the significance of the words used". In *Multicultural Education*, OECD/CERI, Paris, 1987.

19. *Minority* is not the only term to take on numerous forms. The same is true of two others in wide use here, culture and ethnicity; as Raveau comments, these words appear exhausted (Ethnicity, Migrations and Minorities). In *Multicultural Education*, OECD/CERI, *op. cit.*

20. In this connection see the commentary by Françoise Morin on the communication by F.H.M. Raveau, "Ethnicity, Migration and Minorities". In *Multicultural Education*, OECD/CERI, *op. cit.*

21. On the changing picture which a society has of a social reality that in itself does not change, see Sayad's review of the lexical shift by which "minority" comes to refer to what was earlier a set of "immigrants" (Sayad, A., *op. cit.*).

22. Sayad, A.: *op. cit.*, pp. 125-126.

23. Mills, A.: *op. cit.*

24. *Linguistic Minorities in England*. A report by the Linguistic Minorities Project for the Department of Education and Science, Institute of Education, University of London, July 1983.

25. An excellent demonstration, concerning Arabic among the Maghreb population, is given in Grandguillaume, G.: *Arabisation et politique linguistique au Maghreb*, Maisonneuve & Larose, Paris, 1983.

26. The question of the identification of linguistic minorities and membership of a linguistic minority was a problem for researchers on the major British project concerning linguistic minorities, run by the University of London's Institute of Education for the Department of Education and Science

between 1979 and 1983. Given the symbolic value of language and the sentimental nature of ties with it, the researchers based membership of minority linguistic groups on subjective data provided by minority members, *Linguistic Minorities in England*, *op. cit.*

27. On the difficulties of measuring the linguistic indicator, see Raveau, F.H.M., *op. cit.*

28. Australian Institute of Multicultural Affairs: *Annual Report 1983–1984*. Melbourne, 1984.

29. On the political side multiculturalism exorcises two familiar demons of any pluralist society, assimilation and separatism. Hence the ambiguity of the term. It can be taken both as a concealed form of separatism, by assimiliationists, and as a method of assimilation, by separatists. That is the position with Canada's multicultural policy (Roberts, L. and Clifton, R.: "Exploring the Ideology of Canadian Multiculturalism", in *Canadian Public Policy*, Vol. VIII, Winter 1982). In Australia, where there is no risk of a separatist movement, the term is understood differently. The issue here is the quest for a balance between a social cohesion achieved by imposing the social norms of the dominant group on all groups, and equality of opportunity which aims to throw open the opportunities so far reserved for the majority (Smolicz, J.: "Multiculturalism and an overarching framework of values: some educational responses for ethnically plural societies", in *European Journal of Education*, Vol. 19, No. 1, 1984). This dialectic is found in current discussions on multiculturalism throughout the OECD countries.

30. A highly elaborate proposal, combining the two positions by taking multiculturalism as an educational discipline and as an overall approach which inspires and alters the entire curriculum, is presented by Banks in *Teaching Strategies for Ethnic Studies*, 3rd Edition, Allyn and Bacon, Boston, 1984. Banks speaks of ethnic studies, ethnic modification of the total curriculum which is to generate a new curriculum based on fresh assumptions and perspectives, teaching multiethnic perspectives and teaching ethnic cultures, and winds up with a strategy for evaluating ethnic education. He makes a distinction between multicultural education, multiethnic education and ethnic studies. These three complementary concepts generate specific practices and teaching programmes whose assembly in a closely linked package is presented as a proposal for global curriculum reform in a multicultural direction. Banks' book has been very successful in the United States, going into three editions in a few years.

31. This is shown clearly by the definitions attempted by the National Council for Accreditation of Teacher Education (NCATE, 1977). An article published in the *Journal of Teacher Education* expresses the disarray felt by teachers called upon to "do" multiculturalism: "We cannot be expected to teach what we don't know, nor can we be expected to design what we don't understand. This dilemma in the interpretation and application of multicultural education remains one of the most critical problems for teacher education. Until we acquire a knowledge base and philosophical belief system concerning multicultural education, we cannot expect teacher education programmes to be designed and implemented as they should be" (Lindsey, A., "Consensus or Diversity? A grave dilemma in schooling", *Journal of Teacher Education*, July–August 1985).

32. Standing Conference of European Education Ministers: *L'éducation des enfants de migrants. Problèmes et perspectives*. Report by G. Vignaux, Council of Europe, Strasbourg, 1983.

33. Porcher, L.: *The Education of the Children of Migrant Workers in Europe: Interculturalism and Teacher Training*. Council of Europe, Strasbourg, 1981.

34. Alalouf, M.: "La culture d'origine et la culture des migrants". Document DECS/EGT(82)4, Council of Europe, Strasbourg, 1982.

35. Rey Von Allman, M.: Preface to the report by Porcher, L., *op. cit.*

36. Porcher, L.: *op. cit.*

37. Porcher, L.: *op. cit.*

38. Porcher, L.: *op. cit.*

39. Standing Conference of European Ministers of Education, *op. cit.*

40. For an overview of publications on bilingualism and bilingual education, see the bibliography attached to Bratt Paulston's study for CERI (Bratt Paulston, C.: "Linguistic Consequences of Ethnicity and Nationalism in Multilingual Settings", in *Multicultural Education*, OECD/CERI, *op. cit.*). Mackey, W.F., in *Bilinguisme et contact des langues* (Klincksieck, Paris, 1976) presents a comparative study of various forms of bilingual education. Andersson, T. and

Boyer, M., in *Bilingual Schooling in the United States* (National Educational Laboratory Publishers, Austin, 1978), give a detailed description of the United States scene. The nature of bilingualism was described by Mackey, W.F., in "The Description of Bilingualism", in *The Canadian Journal of Linguistics*, No. 7, 1962. Lastly, Siguan, M. and Mackey, W.F. have studied the theoretical problems underlying the different forms of bilingual education in *Education and Bilingualism*, UNESCO, International Education Bureau, Paris, 1986.

41. In Sweden a distinction is made between home language and mother tongue. On the special nature of the mother tongue, see the arguments developed by Illich, S.: *Le travail fantôme*, Seuil, Paris, 1981, and Mackey, W.F.: "Mother tongue education: problems and prospects", in *Perspectives*, Vol. XIV, No. 1, 1984, UNESCO, Paris. On definitions of "mother tongue" it is also useful to consult the chapter by Skutnabb-Kangas, T. on this question in the work *Bilingualism or Not. The Education of Minorities*, Multilingual Matters Ltd., Clevedon, United Kingdom, 1983.

Chapter III

MULTICULTURAL EDUCATION POLICIES
IN THE OECD COUNTRIES

Multicultural education policies are no more than a by–product of educational and cultural policies: the choice of the forms of multicultural education is not entirely free. The nature and organisation of the education system and the general directions of government policy limit the range of possible options. In order to understand the issues underlying multicultural education, we need to know when, how, where and why multicultural education develops within a given education system.

The large–scale introduction in Member country educational systems of multicultural curricula with the mobilisation of a considerable number of specialists and teachers involved a complex preparatory process: setting up of working parties, funding and organisation of research projects, drafting of regulations laying down funding and operational criteria, and pilot experiments. Over and above the variety of responses, the same logic is operating. Here we shall endeavour to reveal this logic[1].

The present chapter describes the origin, introduction and characteristics of multicultural education policies in a number of Member countries. No details are given since much has already been published on the subject; instead, a few points that are significant for understanding the trends and special features of these policies are noted[2]. As a rule, most of the authors who have written on this subject have concentrated on the legal issues and treated the education of minorities as a legal problem, not as an anthropological, or indeed a cultural or an educational one. No account is taken here of the legal aspects of the matter since this would have meant sidetracking into law and considering the different national legal traditions. We have instead tried to clarify the explicit or implicit involvement of cultural policy in the development of multicultural education.

We have summed up the evolutionary development of the multicultural education programmes for each national situation, identified the main forces operating in this area, listed the dominant topics and stated the aims of the policies introduced. These national situations are described in geographical order: first, two Scandinavian countries (Sweden and Finland), where a new problem juxtaposes an old one; then the United Kingdom and Ireland, where the situations combine in a more complicated way; next, we go south to study the case of three Mediterranean countries (Italy, Yugoslavia and Spain) which have inherited historical situations, then to the countries in the South Pacific (Australia and New Zealand) and, finally, to the United States and Canada, whose problems are relatively recent but are not really new.

SWEDEN[3]

Swedish policy in the area of multicultural education has the following features:

i) *Determination and speed* of implementation of multicultural education programmes; the first instrument dealing with multicultural education dates from 1966 and eight years later, in 1974, the basic principles of Swedish policy were clearly defined. Faced with the upheaval caused by the arrival of a large number of immigrants and refugees in a culturally homogenous society, the authorities acted quickly and did not hesitate to spell out the options available to public opinion;

ii) *State leadership*: the central government played a decisive leading role in taking up the challenge posed by the presence of minority groups. All the government institutions concerned were officially consulted and took part in the discussions and analyses undertaken by commissions of enquiry, thus facilitating the emergence of a national consensus on the directions of future policies. The changes in the parliamentary majority in the late 1970s did not modify the aims defined by this process, so that the whole Swedish education programme for ethnic minority groups remained highly coherent. Its aims are as follows: *equality* (minorities have the same rights and the same opportunities as the rest of the population); *freedom of choice* (immigrants can opt to retain their linguistic and cultural identity or to adopt the Swedish way of life, which means that the majority must respect this choice and therefore also accept those who refuse to be assimilated); and *co-operation* (the method of reaching decisions which respect the interests of all, implying *tolerance*, mutual *understanding*, and *solidarity* between minority groups and between majority and minority);

iii) *Consistency*: as already pointed out, the directions and structure of the programme have never been challenged, regardless of changes of government. Having ruled out from the beginning any possibility of a return home or massive departure by migrants, a policy of acceptance and integration was worked out. This policy differed from those pursued by other European countries which had considered such an approach;

iv) *The language issue* is practically an obsession in all documents on the education of ethnic minority groups since it raises a paradoxical issue: how to encourage immigrants to learn Swedish while respecting the freedom of choice of minorities. To overcome this difficulty, an ambitious language policy has been devised which refers neither to a "national language", ambiguous in both linguistic and poltical terms, nor to a "mother tongue", but to a "home language";

v) *The research effort*: the development of a consistent multicultural education policy requires great skill in order to avoid taking poor choices which are bound to causes problems. Sweden has invested a great deal in research on multicultural education in order to provide proper support for its policy. Nevertheless, there seems to be some disparity between the amount of research done and the quality of the results obtained.

All these features combine to define a Swedish style in the introduction of multicultural education, characterised by clarity, transparency, respect of justice and equality. Swedish multicultural education policy provides the example of an explicit and enlightened policy.

FINLAND[4]

As distinct from Sweden, Finland, which has been officially bilingual since 1919, has a long tradition of multicultural education policy, whose main features are as follows:

i) *Stability* and *continuity:* the principles governing this policy and the main standards of enforcement were laid down in 1922 in the Language Act (Spraklag of 1.6.1922), which is still in force after being amended in 1935, 1962 and 1975;

ii) *State leadership*, which protects the Swedish minority and lays down precise rules on the use of the two languages in the public services and education;

iii) *Formal legislation*, which details the rights of the Swedish minority (6 per cent of the population) in order to prevent the disappearance of Swedish from a country in which it has been spoken for the last seven centuries. Thus, officially bilingual communes have two separate linguistic systems: a Swedish–speaking school and a Finnish–speaking school, a different inspector for each school and two school boards. Instruction in the second national language is obligatory during compulsory schooling and higher secondary education. In schools for the Lapp minority in Lapland, instruction is given in Lapp which is used in teaching in proportions specified by law;

iv) *Territorial organisation* of the language system: communes belong to one language system or the other according to the proportion of their inhabitants who speak one of the two official languages. This is comparable in ways to the Belgian system, but without its rigidity, and to that of the Indian reserve but is not stigmatised by the welfare approach. The aim here is to apply the criterion of the separation and territorial confinement of the languages, which operates smoothly everywhere except in Helsinki, where the Swedish and Finnish communities are mixed;

v) *Polarisation of the linguistic problem* with a view to protecting a language regarded as part of the national cultural heritage. The issue for Finnish multicultural education policy is to preserve Swedish in Finland; the problem is maintaining a cultural identity after the language has died out. The solution found seems rigid: in Finland, there are no bilingual schools in which instruction is given in both languages as is the case, for example, in Yugoslavia. Tuition is monolingual everywhere and the teaching language is determined by the linguistic zone in which schools are located.

This solution is both formal and conservative: it reflects an unequal relationship in which an overwhelming majority takes the trouble to defend and protect a historic regional minority.

UNITED KINGDOM[5]

Both situations found in the Scandinavian countries, Sweden and Finland, exist side by side in the United Kingdom: presence of historic minorities possessing territorial status and the irruption on the social landscape of new culturally and linguistically different groups. The English education system is often styled a "national service, locally administered". Responsibility for the detail of provision made in maintained schools is not vested in central government but rests with local education authorities and the governing bodies of individual schools. This flexibility is seen as allowing for full account to be taken of local needs and circumstances. We shall consider the English, Welsh and Scottish systems separately in this brief sketch of the British situation.

England

i) The multicultural problem began to emerge in the 1950s with the arrival of coloured British citizens from the Commonwealth countries. When this influx became macroscopic at the start of the 1970s, the education authorities responded with a first report in 1971, *The Education of Immigrants*, followed in subsequent years by a whole series of other reports. The educational problem was thus only slowly taken into account at the national level.

An important stimulus to developments in multi–cultural education in England has been given in recent years by the publication in 1985 of the Report of the Committee of Inquiry into *The Education of Children from Ethnic Minority Groups (The Swann Report)*. The Committee of Inquiry was established by the central government. On publishing the Report, the Government outlined 3 policy tenets: to raise the performance of all children and to tackle obstacles to higher achievement that are common to all; to ensure that ethnic minority children receive the same educational opportunities as other children; and to promote for all children an awareness of Britain's ethnic diversity so as to encourage tolerance and racial harmony;

ii) As opposed to the Nordic countries, the central government takes a back seat here. The leading role in the English education system is played by local authorities, voluntary groups and local associations. However, the absence of an explicit State policy in this area does not mean that there is just no policy at all. Such a policy is both implicit and indirect and characterised by the deployment of a whole series of special peripheral agencies to draft reports analysing the problems and to suggest solutions. However, the machinery for discussing and adopting the conclusions of these reports is vague. Therefore, the authorities have a wide margin for manoeuvre and are not too closely bound by the agency recommendations that they themselves have commissioned.

In the absence of a strong central education authority, multicultural education programmes are scattered, varied and many. The variety and abundance of initiatives makes up to some extent for the absence of precise official directives;

iii) Compared with other European policies, the United Kingdom was early in adopting a new terminology, substituting the word "minorities" for "migrants" in the early 1970s. This change enables the host society to distinguish itself in a new way from the new cultural and linguistic groups (this was necessary since, from the point of view of nationality, the great majority had a British citizenship); next, it gives the white population a particular identity enabling it to call itself the "majority"; lastly, it makes a reception and integration policy possible which does not depend on the assumption of a return home or departure, as is often the case in Europe, apart from Sweden.

Two concerns dominate the British debate in this area: educational selection, which generally penalises pupils of ethnic minority origin more than native pupils, and racial tensions. Hence the two categories in which most British programmes can be put: compensatory education to make up for socio–cultural handicaps, and anti–racist education to promote better understanding of ethnic communities and to combat racial prejudice. Both the official programmes and research have been geared to these two problems.

In pursuance of these policies specific measures are being taken by central government to improve the response of the education service to ethnic diversity. These include action to ensure that future teachers are equipped by their training to respond to the ethnic and cultural diversity of school pupils; grants for the in–service training of teachers in teaching and the curriculum in a multiethnic society; and the development of specially designed initial training courses to increase the recruitment of teachers from ethnic minority backgrounds. Action is also being taken at the national level to ensure that curricula and examinations take account of the ethnic and cultural diversity of the school population and society at large. Specific grants are also being provided to local education authorities for innovative work in schools related to meeting the educational needs of the ethnic minorities, promoting racial harmony and in other ways preparing pupils and students for life in a multiethnic society. In 1987/88, some 70 projects are receiving support and a further 50 will start in 1988/89.

iv) For many years, the official attitude to the problems raised by multiculturalism has been cautious and reserved. This approach, which has been called at once minimalist and pragmatic, is characteristic of the British approach to multicultural education.

British policy, at national level, is very different from the Swedish one: local rather than State initiative, the implicit rather than the explicit, playing for time rather than immediate action. We see a hands–off policy at work here — almost a dotted line policy — which aims to relieve strains and facilitate integration, attaching great value to the compromises emerging over the course of time.

Wales

The main problem in this region is the preservation and development of an ancient minority culture which is confronted by a majority language and culture. The policy deployed here enables a comparison to be made between the treatment reserved for the territorial minorities and that meted out to the new minorities:

i) The language issue emerged rapidly with the introduction of compulsory State education in 1870 and the Education Act which imposed English as the teaching language despite the fact that 90 per cent of the population spoke Welsh. The autonomy the local authorities were subsequently allowed regarding education did not appreciably change this state of affairs. It was not until 1947 that the first Welsh–speaking State school appeared;

ii) The location of Welsh–speaking schools was geared to the community initiatives of local authorities and teachers, who often spearheaded this movement. But the driving force of the community must not be misunderstood, since the latter is divided on the advisability of teaching Welsh and even more so on its use as a language of instruction;

iii) The Welsh situation points to two aspects: the difficulty, where the linguistic issue is contentious, of applying middle–of–the–road solutions such as bilingual education (in the early 1980s, there were about 50 bilingual schools); and the overriding influence of economic trends: economic variables — social and occupational integration — determine the choice of teaching language, while the evolution of the economic life is responsible for the variations of pressure connected with the language problem.

Scotland

The Scottish educational system is separate from the English: a glance at multicultural education policies in Scotland might therefore be interesting to show whether, in a context which is similar in some respects to the Welsh, this institutional diversity has given rise to a different policy:

i) The Scottish educational system has only recently taken account of the multicultural problem. As in Wales, the compulsory State schooling introduced in 1872 adopted English as the teaching language. The educational autonomy granted in 1918 did not change the attitude of the local education authorities. Two reasons explain this choice: economic underdevelopment, which was an incentive to learn English as an escape from poverty; and the internal logic of the educational system, which persuades people to overestimate the cultural and hence educational value of the dominant language. The evolution of education in Scotland does not therefore differ appreciably from the Welsh although in institutional terms the two education systems are not the same;

ii) In a difficult economic situation, the main concerns of populations and governments are economic, and linguistic demands are set aside: the marginalisation of Gaelic and the absence of a struggle to preserve it demonstrate the validity of this principle. Conversely, the rebirth of interest in this language and the increasing number of people who speak it can also be interpreted as a result of a certain improvement in the general socio–economic situation;

iii) The information on local linguistic practices and linguistic exchanges is insufficient for the preparation of a programme of multicultural education. The complexity of the language situation in Scotland, where an officially monolingual English–speaking context embraces local languages as well as other languages brought in by immigrants, makes more research not only desirable but necessary;

iv) In areas where Gaelic has been preserved, bilingual education is now being introduced, but it is difficult to predict the effect and usefulness of such initiatives for want of suitable socio–linguistic surveys. There is also the problem of linguistic arrangements for new minorities who have settled in Scotland during recent migrations. For the moment, ethnic minority children go to the English–speaking schools where courses in languages and cultures of origin are scarce.

IRELAND[6]

The Irish case is interesting from two viewpoints: one is linguistic and concerns the evolution, preservation and disappearance of a language; the other is educational and concerns the role of the school in passing on, protecting and imposing a language. These two problems occur, moreover, in a complex situation where a culture is being preserved while simultaneously the language expressing that culture is dying out. Furthermore, we have the special case in Ireland, rare in the OECD countries, of a majority which has been colonised. The language problem here is not entirely that of a minority, but rather of the majority.

As far as the present report is concerned, Irish experience suggests the following remarks:

i) The margin of autonomy of the educational systems is small: the major options of education policy are imposed by the political context. The teaching language, which is English, was decided when compulsory schooling was introduced in 1831. It took over 40 years up to 1878 to get Irish included in the curriculum as an optional subject. The first bilingual school opened in 1904. We find the same evolution here as in Scotland and Wales: the local language was only very slowly introduced into the State school curriculum;

ii) The stated objective of current Irish language policy is to preserve and protect the national language, which apart from some exceptions (notably the areas where Irish only is spoken) is neither the main language of communication nor the teaching language. The present programme in Ireland illustrates the importance of the symbolic value of ancestral language education: its inclusion in curricula is an act bereft of utilitarian consideration and almost, one might say, totally disinterested, a celebration of the collective memory's search for vestiges of the nation's roots through its language. The effectiveness of teaching the ancestral language is less important than the fact of actually teaching it: the purpose is not empirical — to encourage or facilitate communication in Irish — but political — to protect and build up the national identity using the symbol of language. Advantage is taken here of the school's function as an institution of cultural legitimation.

iii) The choice and maintenance of English as the main teaching language is in response to an understandable economic imperative. What is worth discussing, on the other hand, is the way Irish is introduced into the curriculum.

Despite the gravity of the national issue in Ireland, the language problem is not given priority in Irish education policy. It is not an essential problem and, in any case, a broad national consensus exists on this point. This may explain the discrepancy between the educational means employed and the official objectives: there is no common measure between the intention to preserve, not to say relaunch, the use of Irish and these means. However, the particular nature of the Irish situation should prompt the authorities to work out special solutions, experiment with alternatives and carry out socio-linguistic research with a view to finding answers that fit the Irish context.

SPAIN

In Spain (40 million inhabitants), Spanish or Castilian is the official State language and the language used by the majority of inhabitants. However, there are other languages that are spoken by a substantial proportion of the population, i.e. Catalan, Galician and Basque, a language of unknown origin and probably the oldest of the languages spoken in Europe today.

i) In sharp contrast with the policy of linguistic unification pursued for centuries by the Spanish State, the present democratic regime recognises the country's cultural and linguistic diversity and both protects and encourages it, thanks in particular to the policy of decentralisation which allows regions with their own language to apply their own language policy in every area, including education.

Current legislation provides that, if Spanish is kept as the language of instruction, the regional language can be included in curricula for a minimum of five hours a week at all levels of education. However, more hours can be allocated to the regional language and it can even be made the main language of instruction. In this case, the requirement is that there should be a minimum amount of instruction in Spanish and that children should have a good knowledge of that language when they finish their compulsory education. The regions have differed in the extent to which they have taken advantage of the possibilities afforded by the law, which represent a radical departure from the situation that existed before;

ii) The developments taking place in Spain must be seen against the background of the radical change in the nature of the State: it is the transition from a dictatorial to a democratic regime that has set in motion the process of political and administrative decentralisation and, with this, recognition of the autonomy of various regions within the country (Catalonia, Galicia, the Basque Country). It is thus the move towards democracy that has been the driving force behind the changes in the concept of the State as the guarantor of national cohesion. These democratic forces have been able to act effectively in the cultural and educational spheres, because they have enjoyed administrative autonomy. These changes, however, have not been uniform, which is proof of the profound transformation in the political system: the process has not been identical everywhere, evolving so to speak at differing speeds and in this way respecting the cultural dynamic of each particular linguistic community. The powers of the various autonomous governments are comparable, but the process of introducing the regional language into the education system has not been carried out at the same pace: while very rapid in Catalonia and the Basque Country, it has been slower and less ambitious in Galicia and the Valencia Region.

Spain thus provides an interesting example of the close link that exists between the development of the linguistic and cultural autonomy of different communities and the form of the political system, an aspect of the question that is ever–present but is more visible here than elsewhere;

iii) Such radical political and cultural changes create major administrative problems, problems which are common to any country that undertakes reforms aimed at decentralising its political system (Italy and France, for example). The division of responsibilities between central government and regional governments involves adjustments of an administrative nature which are essential in order to sustain the process taking place. If these adjustments are not made and if the administrative machinery does not adapt itself to these changes, the reforms are likely to fail. This has not been the case in Spain, but there is no lack of disagreement between maximalists and minimalists as regards the proper degree of political, cultural and linguistic autonomy within the country, and the modernisation and reform of school administration. The operation of decentralising education will have all the more chances of success if it is coupled with the modernisation and reform of educational administration. This question does not directly concern those whose task is to organise language instruction, but its importance is such that it needs to be mentioned here: unless there is an appropriate administrative framework to ensure proper management of these reforms, they are likely to fail.

Another aspect of this is the impact of industrial and economic development on cultural demands for the maintenance and defence of the languages in question. A comparison of the reactions of the different regions in mainland Spain is instructive in this respect: in Catalonia, a wealthy and highly industrialised region, there has been a far more active movement in support of language demands than in Galicia, a rural and somewhat underdeveloped region. The interaction between economic well–being and cultural and linguistic vitality is complex and influenced by several factors, whose operation is by no means properly understood. An excellent example of this is the Basque Country, another of Spain's highly developed regions where, nonetheless, more difficulties were encountered in setting up a programme to promote use of the local language than in Catalonia. In this regard, Spain is an ideal choice as a site for investigation into this question;

iv) The aim of the reforms being introduced in the regions other than Castile, and particularly in Catalonia, is very ambitious: it is to ensure that, by the end of compulsory education, every schoolchild is able to speak the two languages and that teachers and students in secondary and higher education can use whichever language they prefer. In other words, it means going from a monolingual to a bilingual system of education. What is remarkable is the fact that this process began only 10 years ago and is proceeding virtually without conflict.

There is no bitter controversy surrounding this operation, the aim of which is to create a network of bilingual schools in those regions where Castilian is not spoken. This is largely due to the astuteness of the reformers who decided against imposing a particular type of bilingual school, but instead adopted a flexible arrangement whereby, in any one region, there can be schools applying different linguistic models, thus allowing parents' genuine freedom of choice. It should also be stressed that the principle of respecting the children's mother tongue does not mean setting up two separate school systems based on the language spoken in the home. All State primary schools are required to accept any child, whatever its mother tongue. In Catalonia, as in any other Autonomous Region, although schools have adopted different language programmes, they accept children of any mother tongue which, by virtue of this recognition and acceptance of the two languages, implies that the objective is integration. The education system in Spain at present is one vast language laboratory where highly significant, full–scale educational experiments are being carried out. The magnitude of this task and the scope of these reforms would require a substantial progamme of research and painstaking evaluation of the administrative and methodological approaches adopted to help children master two languages. This would be well worth doing in the future.

Probably the most striking fact to emerge from this review of the case of Spain is the enormous variety of linguistic situations and educational projects, despite its being one and the same country with one and the same legal system.

Taken as a whole, the effort being made by Spain to incorporate, within the education system, the language of the State and the language spoken in the different territories represents, in terms of the scope of its objectives and the size of the population concerned, one of the most ambitious attempts ever made to implement a language policy respecting the rights of linguistic minorities.

ITALY[7]

Italy reveals a complex situation where the long presence of several territorial minorities and traditions of communal cultural autonomy affect the political targets of national and linguistic unification.

Even now, in Italy, several territorial minorities are endeavouring to protect their specific cultural and linguistic personality in a relatively young State which has not yet fully achieved the country's linguistic unity. Between these two entities (the State and the ethnic minorities who are more or less Italian–speaking), the school, besieged by various ambitions, is given tasks by both parties which are beyond its powers. The following factors should be noted here:

i) As mentioned above, two problems overlap: achievement of the country's linguistic unity after a century of united history and recognition of the rights of the linguistic minorities. As distinct from what has happened elsewhere, the linguistic tensions have not built up so dramatically, except in a few special cases and for relatively short periods. However, it would be a mistake to assume that this will always be the case. Although it is difficult to imagine that any serious linguistic conflict or conflicts could break out in the future, the educational system will, for its part, probably be required to pay more attention to the linguistic situation by adopting a more pragmatical approach to the question;

ii) In the absence of consistent and continuous action by the central authorities and because the school plays a small part in the process of linguistic unification, the minority communities have hitherto had considerable room for manoeuvre on the cultural level, amplified still further by the recent regionalisation. However, this relatively favourable situation could only be best exploited by the economically thriving communities which also had rich cultural and linguistic traditions. Less privileged or more isolated minorities have found it much more difficult to defend their cultures and languages. Once again, culture and economics closely intertwine;

iii) The existence of several minority groups is precarious today. In most cases these communities are bilingual and bicultural: the situation is one of fact, a modus vivendi aimed at survival, preserving both cultural identity and the local language. By remaining open to the outside, these communities have succeeded in developing strategies of accommodation enabling them to resist and not disappear. A more active role for the school in maintaining and developing those minority languages and cultures which are managing to survive seems interesting, but is not easy to plan, since the possible contribution of education to a community's survival is not obvious. It is probable that the school could have a positive effect, but there is a general tendency to overestimate its impact. At this particular level the Italian context offers a field for experiment and observation that would well repay further research;

iv) The weakness of many minorities and the absence of any heavy–handed political encumbrance could enable the construction of different bilingual education models adapted to the needs of the minorities. Unfortunately, due to lack of resources, knowledge and skills, there have not been any systematically–pursued bilingual education programmes so far. The minorities facing the greatest difficulties or those in the process of disappearing have had to rely on themselves to invent solutions for survival. To develop bilingual education some State support is now inevitable.

Italy continues to be a laboratory for major cultural and linguistic experiments. The weakness of administrative structures, relative inefficiency and bureaucracy have more or less neutralised the centralist ambitions of the State; the tradition of autonomy on the part of local and regional authorities undoubtedly constitutes a favourable context for minorities. However, the economic circumstances of several minority communities are a serious handicap. A policy for the minorities which respects their autonomy while avoiding solutions based on assistance is difficult to conceive, but this is the direction that must be taken if communities with local cultures and languages are to be maintained.

YUGOSLAVIA[8]

The nationality problem and its offshoot, the organisation of a multicultural education policy, attain crisis level in this country. As distinct from every other Member country, in Yugoslavia regulation of the rights of the different nations, nationalities and minorities which make up the Federal Republic is central to education policy and not marginal to it. Recognition of cultural and linguistic differences is an imperative of Yugoslav education policy. A study of the Yugoslav experience is therefore pertinent to every country whose education organisation is likely sooner or later to require modification to allow for ethnic and linguistic pluralism.

i) In this Balkan country, the question of nationalities and minorities is neither a new problem nor an old one on which a new one has been grafted, as is the case elsewhere. The Yugoslav case is the classic one of the Nation State confronted with numerous different minorities. To solve this problem after the Second World War the new Socialist Federal Republic of Yugoslavia adopted innovative methods (following the conclusion of the national liberation struggles) to neutralise the nationalist tensions and risks of conflict between different nationalities, and to encourage the development of harmonious coexistence based on mutual understanding between all parts of the new State. Within this framework an active policy for multicultural education was developed;

ii) Education policies, including multicultural ones, contribute to bringing about a new society by allowing the free development, on a basis of equality, of all the nations, nationalities and minorities which make up the country. This project is based on the conviction that education can produce a new type of citizen and eliminate the prejudices of the past. Education thus occupies an important place in political priorities. It may nevertheless be asked whether the educational ambitions constantly reiterated in official declarations do not also engender a certain inability to face up to reality;

iii) Yugoslav multicultural education policy aims to demonstrate that cultural and linguistic diversity is possible within one and the same legal framework and to combine unity with difference while avoiding uniformity. The obsession with formal recognition of the rights of minorities is responsible in the educational sphere for a very complex and detailed body of regulations. The obverse side to this set of rules, some aspects of which are notable for their attachment to protecting the rights of each group, is the rigidity of the solutions, adopted in most cases according to the principle of territoriality;

iv) The attention paid to the organisation of an educational system that recognises cultural and linguistic diversity reveals the power of the cultural factors which constitute a force for both cohesion and disaggregation. The Yugoslav model is characterised by the value it has placed on links between individuals and their community of origin, and has led to an education policy which scrupulously regulates the rights of minorities in the education system.

There is no denying that the Yugoslav model has been quite successful. The solutions adopted, such as the introduction of bilingual education in Slovenia or Voivodina, are experiments which must be closely followed in order to draw general conclusions that might be of use elsewhere.

NEW ZEALAND[9]

Although it is tempting to treat the New Zealand case as a special example of a policy introduced for ancient aboriginal populations, this would be erroneous. As distinct from what happens elsewhere, the aborigine population here (the Maoris) is not confined in reservations but is highly urbanised and mixed with the white population.

This situation affects the terminology: instead of multicultural education, the New Zealanders prefer to speak of bicultural education, thus referring to the daily exchange between Aborigines and the population of European origin. The importance of this confrontation is not only cultural; it is also economic. Two different types of economic organisation, the organisation of majority white society and the tribal organisation of minority Maori society, are responsible for practices and attitudes which have nothing to do with the influence of multicultural education. The multicultural education policy deployed so far has the following features:

i) The question of multicultural education arose fairly recently, in the 1950s. At that time it was clear that it was no longer possible to continue with an education policy imbued with the cultural traditions of the majority of European origin. In the absence of special action programmes, the native population, disadvantaged in economic, social, educational and health terms, was likely, after having nearly died out altogether, to become an acute social problem;

ii) Because the organisation of the educational system is centralised, the State is influential in the change of direction now beginning to take place. It is the

State which consults the community bodies, sets up commissions, funds reports and supports research. Closer analysis of this change might help in understanding the reactions of the educational and political systems to the redefinition of the cultural function of the school;

iii) New Zealand policy wavers between two different objectives: one, which might be regarded as an ethnic policy objective, concerns the survival of Maori society; the other, relating to cultural policy, aims to transform New Zealand into a bicultural society. In neither case is the school free to choose: it can but assist in effecting the political outcome of the democratic process. It is relatively easy to organise ethnic education, since the authorities are familiar with compensatory education; the introduction of bicultural education for the whole of New Zealand society raises far more problems and in particular encounters considerable resistance among part of the white population;

iv) Educational solutions cannot in themselves overcome the inequality suffered by the Maori community. The introduction of Maori language teaching and the improvement of schooling for Maori pupils will no doubt have long–term effects but one might query the validity of a strategy limited to the inclusion of Maori language courses in curricula. The introduction of bicultural education for the majority of the population is under study; the problems this raises are not only practical and political but also of considerable theoretical importance and have to be tackled in order to avoid lapsing into mere folklore. Future experiment and research should turn in this direction.

The circumstances in New Zealand create favourable conditions for an original multicultural education policy whose development is not only unhampered by separatist movements but also supported by a strong desire for integration in a bicultural society. The use of solutions tried elsewhere must be considered with caution, while an innovative effort is necessary to find special arrangements to fit the local context.

AUSTRALIA[10]

The situation in Australia is more complex than that in New Zealand for two reasons.

Firstly, the indigenous population (the Aborigines) is much more linguistically and culturally varied than are the Maori people of New Zealand. Some one hundred and fifty languages are still spoken by Aboriginal and Torres Strait Islander Australians, although only a much smaller number is considered viable. The previous policies of assimilation of Aborigines — and the effect of destruction of their cultural and linguistic background — have been at least partially reversed. There are now significant and concerted efforts to restore pride in Aboriginal traditional life and to maintain indigenous languages. Aborigines live in a wide variety of socio–cultural contexts. Those in isolated and rural areas have frequently been able to retain their traditional culture. Those in urban environments have tended to live on the margins of society. For Aboriginal and Torres Strait Islander people education, and bicultural and bilingual education as a part of multicultural policies, generally aims to achieve improvements in their extremely low educational success rates.

Secondly, the post–World War II migration programme has brought permanent settlers to Australia from well over one hundred countries speaking a wide range of languages. After Israel, Australia has the highest proportion of its population born overseas. A high proportion of these immigrants have been non–English speaking. The source countries have been diversifying rapidly. The main reasons for the migration programme have been: the boom in manufacturing industry requiring a labour force after 1947; the perceived need for population growth for a wide range of economic and strategic reasons; and humanitarian acceptance of refugees and displaced persons.

Although minorities comprise about a quarter of the population, it was not until the early 1970s that concerted government intervention in schooling was enacted. In the late 1960s and early 1970s there was agitation for the setting up of services and programmes to teach English as a second language to the new arrivals and to provide interpretation and translation services. These were the first initiatives in what was to evolve as a broadly–accepted public policy of multiculturalism:

i) From the initial stress on providing services to enhance equality of opportunity in education for the new arrivals, Australian state governments initiated cultural awareness programmes and mother–tongue teaching programmes to bolster the ethnic identity of young children of immigrant background and to promote inter–ethnic tolerance. A large number of government–sponsored reports called for the extension of programmes in multicultural education. Successive governments through the 1970s extended these initiatives although they tended to remain *ad hoc* and localised;

ii) After 1978 Commonwealth (federal) government initiatives were taken to bolster the teaching of ethnic community languages in the education system, to integrate parents into decision–making structures and to evolve curricula for all students in which the idea of cultural pluralism was promoted as beneficial and natural to Australia. The previous stress on equality for ethnic minorities was modified to stress cultural tolerance and sharing among Australians of different backgrounds. This was built around adherence to certain "core elements" of Australian identity, such as the acceptance of English as the common national language;

iii) Australia's conception of multicultural education now tends to gravitate between these two poles; at one extreme there are programmes whose purpose and justification are to ensure equality of achievement and opportunity for cultural minorities; at the other extreme there is an emphasis on the enrichment of Australian society through diversity. In addition, the elements of incorporating Aboriginal perspectives in curricula as well as perspectives deriving from Australia's place in Asia are attracting significant attention. There is great variety among the different states and in some states schools are relatively autonomous.

iv) The following features have now been accepted as part of the Australian approach:

   a) Universal proficiency in English but the retention of cultural values and lifestyles which diverge from the dominant ones;
   b) Commitment to the achievement of equality of educational attainment for disadvantaged minorities, especially Aborigines;
   c) The evolution of curriculum practices which reflect and value the diversity of the society and promote tolerance and acceptance;
   d) The setting up of programmes to teach second languages, with significant stress on ethnic community and Aboriginal languages, key languages of Asia and languages of geo–political importance to the nation.

In many respects Australia has been one of the most innovative countries in multicultural education and has tried in recent years to design its initiatives with all children in mind. Although many groups of ethnic minority background do well at school and attain conspicuous educational success, there are still many unsolved problems and practice often lags behind policy. Nevertheless, the adoption and funding of a National Policy on Languages which builds on multicultural initiatives augurs well for the future.

A diversity of programmes exists at state and federal level to support ethnic schools: integrated mother–tongue teaching; second language and bilingual teaching; parent involvement; and culturally pluralist curricula. Comprehensive policies have been adopted to guide these programmes and, although many individuals and groups are opposed to multiculturalism, a broad consensus exists about it, in society and at a political level. Education plays the central role in multicultural policies in attempting to forge a pluralism built around social cohesion and adherence to core values.

CANADA[11]

To attempt to summarise the multicultural education policies in Canada is practically impossible since Canada does not have a single education policy let alone a single multicultural education policy. The ten Canadian provinces have full power over educational matters: each of them has evolved its own institutions and structures, even though there are numerous similarities between them.

   i) The inclusion in education policies of multicultural issues did not come about without difficulty and is relatively recent. Unanimity as to the multicultural nature of Canada has been achieved gradually and is well established today. Hon. Jack Murta, former Minister of State for Multiculturalism stated in 1984 in his opening speech to the Second National Conference on Multicultural and Intercultural Education in Toronto that "cultural and racial diversity constitutes the very essence of Canadian identity", and the former Minister of Education for Nova Scotia, Hon. Terence Donahoe, emphasized in his closing speech to the same conference that there was no future for Canada other than as a multicultural country.

50

The term "multicultural" came into common use in Canada in 1971 when the then Prime Minister, Rt.Hon. Pierre Trudeau, stated the policy of "multiculturalism within a bilingual framework". This policy was set up slowly. The first province to enact legislation recognising multiculturalism was Saskatchewan in 1974. By 1986, only three provinces had passed similar legislation. However, this does not give the whole picture: in practice, at federal as well as at provincial and local levels, there have been innumerable initiatives and programmes inspired by multiculturalism and reflecting cultural and linguistic diversity.

ii) The impetus for this development derives from three sources: government, the ethnic communities, and educators.

The inquiries of the federal Royal Commission on Bilingualism and Biculturalism, which held public meetings across Canada in the late 1960s, aroused widespread interest in the issues of language and culture, and drew attention to the existence in Canada of a pluralistic society — in effect, giving intercultural relations a higher profile. Public debate was stimulated, and minority groups became more conscious of their particular needs and aspirations.

The provinces developed a variety of procedures for dealing with the reality of multiculturalism, such as forming advisory councils (e.g. the Ontario Advisory Council on Multiculturalism and Citizenship and the Alberta Heritage Council) and interministerial committees concerning multiculturalism. Several provinces sponsored major conferences, inviting representatives of ethno–cultural groups and developing a variety of recommendations, some of which related to education. In most provinces, new government ministries and agencies were established and various policy documents were prepared, advocating equal access to government services and urging social justice for all. These policy statements served as a basis for educators in determining appropriate responses to multiculturalism for schools.

Generally, only policies governing the use of language have been written into law. Other aspects of multicultural programmes are expressed in statements of educational philosophy or in curriculum guidelines. Although materials have been produced in abundance, provincial policy statements focusing specifically on multicultural education remain largely in the process of development. Large urban school boards, however, do have written policy statements applying to their particular jurisdictions; examples include Halifax, Montreal, Toronto, Winnipeg, Saskatoon, Edmonton and Vancouver.

In general, the history of multicultural education in the provinces has been shaped by several factors: the legal right of official minority–language students to education in their mother tongue; the desire of recent immigrants to have their children learn English or French; the desire of Native peoples for education in their own language and for knowledge of their own cultures; the interest of ethnic communities in their cultural heritage, and in the bilingual education.

iii) Although at present no province has issued a definitive policy statement devoted exclusively to multicultural education, government positions on its various aspects have been presented in official education documents. Furthermore, policy can usually be inferred from the kinds of measures adopted by provincial ministries/departments of education. Judging from the foregoing, a high degree of similarity exists in regard to the central themes and principal goals of multicultural education. This is a striking proof of the consensus as to the policy function of the school and the view taken of Canadian society.

Analysis of official statements and of the range of multicultural education initiatives reveals three principal themes: bilingualism and the safeguard of heritage languages; relations between ethnic groups; the struggle against racism. Since 1971 Canada has applied a policy of official bilingualism in a multicultural context. This trend produced an intense research activity and experimentation in the teaching of languages in schools and curricula have been modified to provide instruction in either of Canada's two official languages to Francophones or Anglophones when they constitute a numerical minority in a particular province. It is undeniable that Canadian education authorities have made a considerable effort over the last 20 years in regard to language teaching.

Next to the linguistic problems, the theme that has been given most attention in multicultural education has been relations between ethnic groups, knowledge of the cultures of the other communities and intercultural exchanges. In this field, the inventiveness of Canadian educators is impressive, but the most interesting political aspect for a foreign observer is perhaps the close collaboration that Education Ministers of several provinces have established with the provincial human rights commissions. This approach deserves to be pointed out since it gives multicultural education a broader standpoint than that normally adopted and serves as a protective barrier against the dangers of cultural relativism.

Lastly, like what is happening in the United Kingdom, another theme has emerged as an important issue in consideration of multicultural education in Canada, i.e. the struggle against racism and the need to educate children against racial prejudice and discrimination. The immigration by people who are no longer mainly white and the repercussions of racial problems such as those in the United States have helped move multicultural education issues in this direction.

iv) Linguistic policy, multicultural education and the safeguard of the cultural identity of ethnic groups have been at the centre of policy discussions in Canada. The underlying reason for all this is to be found in the constitution of the country itself, and in its geographical and human components. It is possible that the size of the country, the sharp contrasts of all kinds, the diversity of the cultural fabric, economic and linguistic imbalances, as well as the weight of tradition are all potential causes of instability which need to be balanced or neutralised with an appropriate political organisation able to insure the national cohesion. Centrifugal forces are not really a threat and the likelihood of fragmentation of the country does not exist any more; the danger is more insidious and concealed. The desire for autonomy and independence which constitutes the strength of local and provincial political life is not easy to reconcile with some common political framework associated with the European concept of the state, by the development of the modern economy and by the pressures of international competition. The linguistic and cultural problem is at the heart of this debate, as it is in the quest for a consensus sufficiently powerful to hold together (and even appeal to) the component elements of the country, while at the same time being sufficiently flexible to allow local and provincial bodies a high degree of autonomy. Culture can serve as this binding element by being both strong and weak at the same time. It allows for respect for diversity while forging solidarity and a new type of unity whose foundations are not those of the traditional nation state.

Multicultural education in Canada comprises a wide range of experimentation. This mixture is surprising since it contains the latest innovations (immersion programmes) and various experiments in bilingual teaching, where one official language and a heritage language are used at one and the same time as teaching languages (e.g. bilingual English–Ukranian courses in Alberta, in Saskatchewan and in Alberta where bilingual English–Hebrew and English–German courses are found).

This variety of achievements illustrates the flexibility of the Canadian education systems. The single weak point is perhaps a certain propensity towards an activism that may inhibit objective analysis and conceptual clarity. It nevertheless remains that in some Canadian provinces it has been possible to overcome one of the most commonly encountered educational taboos (outside Canada) by accepting the use of a non–official language as a language of instruction, thus opening the way to original bilingual teaching experiments which have to be followed and known.

UNITED STATES[12]

It is no easy matter to sketch a profile of United States multicultural education policy and to interpret the present trends since there are so many actors involved that we might never get more than a partial view of what is going on. We merely note some of the main landmarks here:

i)   Direct Federal Government intervention in multicultural education is relatively recent and began in the 1960s, coinciding with the period of the civil rights struggle. The history of the adoption of multicultural education is therefore marked by social concerns arising from the problems of minority integration. There is a link between the expansion of the welfare policies at the time of the war on want and the development of multicultural education, and this has given a "welfare" colouring to these educational programmes which they have not yet lost;

ii) The introduction and evolution of multicultural education policies in the United States have been heavily influenced by many lobbies (the black community, the Hispanics, etc.) and within each community by several types of militants, including professional educators. But it would be a mistake to believe that the communities put up a united front to support their educational demands: their interests diverge and there is no unanimity in this connection even within each community;

iii) The implementation of bilingual education programmes is highly controversial due to the ambiguity of the objectives assigned to this type of instruction. Education departments, at both Federal and State level, are not against bilingual education as such, provided it moves in the direction of assimilation: the organisation of home language and culture courses should continue to be a means of equalising educational opportunities and helping minorities to do better at school and integrate more easily into American society. However, some groups feel that ethnic instruction must not only serve to facilitate or speed up the teaching of English to children who have an imperfect knowledge of it because they speak other languages in the home, but should also be a means of safeguarding minority cultures. This basic disagreement regarding objectives to a large extent explains the problems encountered by multicultural education in the United States;

iv) There are two central issues to the debate: bilingual education and equal opportunities. These cannot be dissociated. Bilingual education was originally proposed as a means of obtaining better school performance from non–English–speaking children. After several years of bilingual education, the argument as to how bilingual education should be organised and how effective it is compared to other educational models is still far from resolved. There is a particular resistance to transitional bilingual education programmes which use the home language rather than English as the language of instruction at the beginning of schooling, teach English as the second language and gradually move over to instruction in English as children's skills in that language improve.

American policy had the merit of putting the problem in utilitarian terms and this is well. There is a symbolic usefulness in putting minority group languages into the curricula and there is also a pragmatic usefulness in doing so for they do not necessarily coincide. If bilingual education is to have a better future, these two interests must converge: bilingual education can be accepted on a vast scale if it offers improved chances of educational success, which is the necessary prerequisite for social and occupational integration.

NOTES AND REFERENCES

1. Churchill, S.: *The education of linguistic and cultural minorities in the OECD countries.* Multilingual matters, Clevedon, 1986.
2. Among the main publications providing information on the various countries' programmes, it will be useful to consult: the *World Yearbook of Education 1981* (Megarry, Nisbet, Hoyle, eds.,

1981); the *Harvard Encyclopedia of American Ethnic Groups* (Thornstrom, Orlow, Handlin, eds., 1980); and the CERI/OECD study on *The Education of Minority Groups. An Enquiry into Problems and Practices of Fifteen Countries* (Gower Publishing Company, Ltd., Aldershot, England, 1983).

3. Swedish policy on immigration and multicultural education has been defined essentially in the following three reports: Inrikesdepartementet: "Arbetsmarknadspolitik", SOU 1965:9 (Labour market policy, 1965); Ecklesiastikdepartementet: "Skolgang borta och hemma", SOU 1966: 55 (Schooling abroad and at home, 1966); and Arbetsmarknadsdepartementet: "Invandrarutredningen 3", Invandrarna och minoriteterna, SOU 1974: 69 (Immigrants and minorities, Report No. 3, 1974).

   For details of multicultural education policy, see: Fris, A.M.: "Policies for minorities education: A comparative study of Britain and Sweden", Ph.D. dissertation, University of Stockholm, 1982; the article by Opper, S.: "Multiculturalism in Sweden: a case of assimilation and integration", in *Comparative Education*, Vol. 19, No. 2, 1983; and the study by Bratt Paulston, C.: "Swedish research and debate about bilingualism. A report to the National Swedish Board of Education", National Swedish Board of Education, Stockholm, 1982.

4. The main source on Finnish policy for the Swedish minority was: the report by the National Board of General Education drafted for the CERI/ECALP project, research reports No. 21, 1979, No. 24, 1981, and No. 26, 1980 by the Centre for Research in Comparative Sociology of the University of Helsinki; as well as two studies by Allardt: Allardt, E., Miemois, K.J.: "The Swedish-speaking minority in Finland. Research reports", Research Group for Comparative Sociology, University of Helsinki, 1981 , and Allardt, E.: "A minority in both centre and periphery. An account of the Swedish-speaking Finns", *European Journal of Political Research*, No. 10, 1982.

5. There is a plethora of publications on multiculturalism and multicultural education policies in the United Kingdom. Some studies are particularly valuable and a number of official documents provide essential information on all of the current trends, including:

   A.A., 1984: "Race, education and research. Rampton, Swann and after". Centre for Multicultural Education and the Thomas Coram Research Unit. Working Paper No. 3. University of London, Institute of Education.

   Cohen, G., 1984: "The politics of bilingual education", in *Oxford Review of Education*. Vol. 8, No. 2, 1984.

   Dorn, A., Troyna, B., 1984: "Multiracial education and the politics of decision-making", in *Oxford Review of Education*. Vol. 8, No. 2, 1984.

   Grant, N., 1983: "Multicultural education in Scotland", in *Comparative Education*. Vol. 19, No. 2, 1983.

   ILEA, 1983: "Race, sex and class. Multi-ethnic education in schools". ILEA, County Hall, London.

   Linguistic Minorities Project, 1983: "Linguistic minorities in England. A report for the Department of Education and Science". University of London, Institute of Education, London.

   McLean, M., 1981: "Comparative approaches to multiculturalism and education in Britain". Centre for Multicultural Education. *Occasional Paper No. 3*. University of London, Institute of Education, London.

   McLean, M., 1983: "Education and cultural diversity in Britain: Recent immigrant groups", in *Comparative Education*. Vol. 19, No. 2, 1983.

   Orzechowska, E., 1984: "What it means to be a bilingual child in Britain today". Centre for Multicultural Education. Working Paper No. 4. University of London, Institute of Education, London.

   Rampton, A., 1981: *West Indian children in our schools*. HMSO, London.

   Rosen, H., 1980: "Language and literacy: Education for multicultural societies: England and Wales". CERI/OECD, Paris (document for internal use only).

   Schools Council, 1982: "Education of children from ethnic minority groups". Schools Council Pamphlet 19, London.

Swann Report, 1985: *Education for All*. Report of the Committee of Inquiry into the Education of Children from Ethnic Minority Group. HMSO, London.

Taylor, M.J., 1981: *Caught between. A review of research into the education of pupils of West Indian origin*. NFER–Nelson, London.

6. On the teaching of Irish in Ireland, see Harris, J.: "Spoken Irish in primary schools. An analysis of achievements". Institinuid Teangeolaiochta Eireann, Dublin, 1984. Concerning Irish education policy, the article by O'Buachalla: "Educational policy and the role of the Irish language from 1831 to 1981", *European Journal of Education*, Vol. 19, No. 1, 1984, contains an interesting bibliography.

7. The annex to the Italian report for the CERI/ECALP project gives an exhaustive bibliography on the minority groups in Italy. Other information is provided in: Di Iorio, F. (ed): *L'educazione plurilingue in Italia*, CEDE, Frascati, 1983; Meghnagi, S.: *Lingua, cultura, educazione. Tutela delle minoranze*, Materiali e documenti, Ed. Sindacale Italiana, Rome, 1982; Bettelheim, P., Benedikta, R.: *Apartheid in Mitteleuropa? Sprache und Sprachenpolitik in Südtirol*, Jugend und Volk, Vienna 1982.

8. The information on Yugoslav policy comes from the Yugoslav report for the CERI/ECALP project and from the collected acts of the Ljubljana seminar organised jointly by CERI and the Yugoslav authorities in October 1985: "Razprave in Gradivo 18" (Treatises and Documents No. 18): Education in multicultural societies. Institute for Ethnic Studies, Ljubljana, 1986.

9. For New Zealand multicultural education policy, see the report by the New Zealand Department of Education for the CERI/ECALP project, the annual reports from the Department of Education to Parliament, the report by the Race Relations Conciliators: "Race against time", Human Rights Commission, Wellington, 1982, the same Commission's report on "Racial harmony in New Zealand. A statement of issues", Wellington, 1982, the report on the Conference on Priorities in Multicultural Educational Research, held in Wellington in 1980 (Department of Education, Wellington, 1981) and the reports by the Advisory Committee for Maori Education.

10. The official Australian report drafted for the CERI/ECALP project by the Australian Ministry of Education and Youth Affairs together with the Schools Commission describes the position in Australia, trends in multicultural education policy, the present thinking of the Australian authorities in this area and the organisation of multicultural education. Poole, E., in the article on "Educational opportunity for minority groups. Australian research reviewed", published in the *World Yearbook of Education*, 1984, gives an overview of Australian research on multicultural and bilingual education and linguistic problems.

There is a very large bibliography on this issue in Australia which has been partly commented on by Craven, E.: *Multilingualism and education. An annotated bibliography*. Education Research and Development Committee. ERDC Report No. 25, Australian Government Publishing Service, Canberra, 1980; unfortunately, this study is now out of date. The Australian Institute for Multicultural Affairs on the state of multicultural and migrant education describes the new direction taken after 1979 (*Review of multicultural and migrant education*. Australian Institute for Multicultural Affairs, Melbourne, 1980). Harris' work on ethnic identity and the role of the concept of identity in the discussion on the organisation of multicultural education dates from the same period (Harris, J.: *Identity: A study of the concept in education for a multicultural Australia*. ERDC Report No. 22, Canberra, 1980). Another report by the Australian Institute for Multicultural Affairs (1982) on the programmes and services for migrants is particularly interesting since it is one of the rare examples of an evaluation of the initiatives taken (*Evaluation of post-arrival programmes and services*. Australian Institute for Multicultural Affairs, Melbourne, 1982). The 89 recommendations proposed in conclusion to this evaluation are most interesting. Lastly, a critical introduction to ethnic schools is provided by the study by Kringas, P. and Lewins, F.: *Why ethnic schools?* Australian National University Press, Canberra, 1980.

11. The information given is taken primarily from the report "Multicultural Education Policies in Canada" of September 1986 which the Canadian Council of Education Ministers prepared at the request of CERI.

12. The American bibliography is enormous. The information given here is based on the main ideas set out in the report by Glazer, N.: "Cultural Differences and Equality of Educational Achievement", published by OECD/CERI in *Multicultural Education*, Paris, 1987.

Chapter IV

THE ISSUES IN THE DEBATE
ON MULTICULTURAL EDUCATION

The picture of multicultural education policies given in this report makes it possible to bring out some interesting similarities and differences. Their implementation seems to be conditioned by four main parameters:

— The drive inherent in cultural processes;
— The impact of political values;
— Changes within teaching systems;
— The socio–economic context.

Almost all teaching systems function in societies that are in fact culturally complex, hybrid, heterogeneous and pluralist. How can these factors be accounted for in these teaching systems? Should they be taken into account? Education systems are not culturally neutral, since the store of knowledge which forms the subjects taught is based on a set of criteria that are culturally connotative, and teaching practices (the way a class is organised, for example) are shaped by forms of socialisation prevailing outside the school. The same is true of the perception of multicultural action. The relevance of these perceptions, which serve as references for the production of curricula, has therefore to be examined. The current interest in multicultural education coincides with a tendency to revise these perceptions.

State schools have always had a political role to play in inculcating patriotic values and providing initiation into the political system. In many countries the social changes in recent years have been felt as a danger for national traditions. This explains the renewed interest in the political function of schools, in civic instruction and in education in democratic values, i.e. in teaching which is in no way ambiguous so far as the basic principles of democratic life are concerned. Multicultural education programmes (although not seen as part of civic education), since they are unfortunately too often aimed at a minority rather than at all children, nevertheless fit into this picture to the extent that they teach about a just and tolerant society in which human rights are respected.

From a strictly educational viewpoint, the inequality of educational opportunity affecting most minority groups is one of the most serious problems to be solved by multicultural education policies. The action taken through equal opportunity policies in education has not come up to expectations; we refer here to changes in the requirements for admission to the education system, changes in teaching structures, improvement in the quality of equipment and especially in teaching methods, the development of compensatory programmes, the creation of special classes, and the greater number of induction, assistance and language courses. The equality achieved in the teaching conditions has contributed only slightly to greater equality in educational results. Despite the use of a wide range of resources, educational systems have been unable substantially to reduce inequality of opportunity. Accordingly, if we keep to the present organisational scheme for teaching, no rapid improvement seems likely in the short term in the average educational standards of pupils from ethnic minority groups.

The objective of the changes planned for educational systems is to strike a balance between a series of dichotomous positions — in other words, to find educational solutions which would avert the dangers likely to affect the system of social relationships prevailing in a given society and which, at the same time, would encourage the social integration of ethnic minority groups.

From this viewpoint, multicultural education stands on the line separating the two main trends of the development of education systems, namely the move towards uniformity on the one hand and the emphasis on respect for and encouragement of individual differences on the other. For a long time education policies aimed at uniformity: the idea was to treat everyone in the same way, have everyone learn the same language, offer them the same services, instil the same values and impart the same knowledge. This strategy was inspired by a concern for justice and equality, but also by the need to promote and safeguard the social consensus. It would be wrong to underestimate this aspect of the matter: the assimilationist policies in education, which were applied explicitly until the 1960s in most Member countries, were intended to consolidate national unity. Schools were seen as a melting pot where differences should have and could have been eliminated. Today it is difficult to imagine this consensus, for the same concern over damage to or even break–up of the State or nation is no longer felt, although it cannot be said that the perception of this threat has really disappeared.

It would therefore be a mistake to judge former policies in the light of current attitudes and criticise them for being intolerant of the cultural differences, traditions and aspirations of ethnic minorities. Admittedly they were, but with a precise purpose, which was to build a new society, and they should be judged above all in relation to their objective. It is, moreover, the same goal — safeguarding or strengthening national cohesion or the country's unity — which has set educational policies on the opposite track whereby cultural differences are now recognised, as is obviously the case in Australia, New Zealand or Canada where the advocates and theorists of multicultural education emphasize the need to bring out the similarities rather than the differences between cultures. Teaching systems have always been called upon to contribute to the creation of national unity, and this continues to be the case.

For example, special teaching exclusively reserved for immigrants' children or ethnic minority groups has been strongly opposed in the United Kingdom, for it was seen as a potentially divisive factor that could have led to cases of educational apartheid[1]. In the United States, doubts about bilingual programmes are partly due to similar fears[2]: those arguing in favour of maintaining cultural differences are suspected of rejecting the melting–pot and of refusing to integrate with American society, i.e. of having aims which the vast majority of the population refuse to countenance[3]. Some of that population see the demands of the Hispanics as pointing the way to the break–up of the country and the end of a myth, which partly explains the coolness of public support for policies promoting bilingualism[4].

In recent official pronouncements in several countries on multicultural education the same central idea recurs: the progress represented by the development of democratic pluralist societies considered to be the least imperfect model for the coexistence of social groups with differing economic and cultural interests. In other words, the real goal of multicultural policies is the coexistence within the same State of different communities which share among themselves on some fair and agreed basis the jointly–produced wealth and means of subsistence.

From this viewpoint, the problem of multiculturalism has been formulated with clarity in Canada where for years an attempt has been made to work out a strategy that would counterbalance assimilationist and separatist propensities. Although it was easy to understand that the policies for protecting or promoting the interests of ethnic minorities could be a threat to national integrity when they were taken to the extreme, it was more difficult to concede that the opposite policy (which made no allowance for the specific cultural and linguistic characteristics of ethnic minorities) was also a threat to society as a whole. This was observed by the Honourable James Fleming, Canadian Minister of State for Multiculturalism in 1981[5].

The social consensus

The role of education is supposed to be to make all citizens understand the necessity and advantages of an open system that permits a balanced mix of autonomy and constraints for all ethnic groups (including the majority group) so as to maintain and strengthen national cohesion. In all countries, multicultural policy is intended to set up or safeguard a consensus among all the parties involved with regard to a type of social contract that will make coexistence within a common socio–economic system attractive to the majority as well as the minorities. There is no doubt that this consensus is mainly achieved by social justice and not by education. In this respect education plays only a minor, symbolic role, which in no way means that this role is irrelevant or should be underestimated[6].

The fact remains that, if the harmonious coexistence of culturally and economically different groups is to be achieved, all communities must feel that they are obtaining some benefit from this situation. In other words, the distribution of wealth must not be too uneven. From this viewpoint, in contemporary societies with extensive social security systems, income distribution policy and participation in the social welfare system can act as a regulatory factor in coexistence and integration. As the former Canadian Minister of State Mr. Fleming says, multiculturalism works if it means "the right to equality of opportunity", or the right "to feel equal in a pluralist society"[7]. A real multiracial society cannot be achieved, according to the Bradford municipal authorities, except through equality, i.e. equality of treatment, equality of opportunity and equality of services.

To neutralise racism, xenophobia and inter–community violence, pluralist society must be to some extent attractive and advantageous, forming a kind of community of interests within which individuals may, if they so wish, take advantage of their special ethnic characteristics[8]. If, however, social welfare is inadequate or ill–adjusted, if the chances of making money remain limited, if the prospects for progress or social advancement are slight, and if inequality in education remains pronounced, then the risk of conflicts becoming more serious increases, particularisms become more accentuated and ethnicity is overstressed[9]. It is used to justify envy, jealousy and violence as a means of obtaining some of the wealth or wellbeing which has been withheld and also of gaining some respect or recognition which is felt to be lacking. Ethnicity (ethnic demands) becomes an outlet or a form of redemption making up for the lack of something else.

The cultural identity

How can the development of multicultural educational programmes be explained from this viewpoint? What purpose do they serve? What is their function? Two approaches can be seen in this respect, which may coexist or be mutually exclusive: in one case, multicultural education has a political function with a collective finality; in the other, it has an educational function with an individual finality.

In the individual context, multicultural education is intended to prevent the damage done by academic failure among children in ethnic minority groups. According to a widely held view, this failure is often psychological; its underlying causes are considered to be a weakening of the self–image, lack of self–confidence and a depreciating perception by the pupil of his own identity. To show that in objective terms the language or moral and social codes of the ethnic community to which the pupil belongs are not depreciated is of no help, since the difficulties experienced are personal and subjective, and affect emotions and judgements[10]. Educational failure of minority children is attributed partly to a weakening of the personality due to an accumulation of various factors within and outside the school, both subjective and social. If this analysis is correct educational work should aim to counteract the causes of pupils' instability, restore their self–confidence and strengthen their personalities or "empower" them.

Some writers think that multicultural education programmes should give priority to the psychological development of children from ethnic minority groups[11], encourage them to express themselves, and strengthen their psycho–emotive stability[12] by providing adjustment and remedial courses. Schools are thus expected to fulfil what is practically a therapeutic function. Considering the limitations of schools in this respect, it may be asked whether this ambition is appropriate and whether schools can take such action and assume such a heavy responsibility. Excessive numbers of children of immigrants in special education classes in Europe are a good illustration of the way the situation can get out of hand when schools venture onto the uncertain ground of therapy: differences are liable to be perceived as anomalies[13].

Multicultural education is not only concerned with individual identity: for many experts the collective identity is at least as important as the individual one[14]. One of its functions is thought to be to help rediscover the culture of origin, to maintain, strengthen and perhaps create the feeling of belonging to a community and of respect for ethnic values. Many instruments and declarations relating to multicultural education are expressed in these terms. To this end, respect for tradition and customs, exploitation of founding mythology, celebration of the national genius and its outstanding achievements and historical figures are used to encourage a sense of pride in belonging to a great nation enabled to excel by its special talents and culture. Such greatness is automatically reflected in each member of the community and helps maintain its identity. The danger of becoming locked into a kind of ethnic fatality should not be underestimated when asserting the primacy of the community over the individual. In the intentions of some of the promoters and advocates of multicultural education this danger is clearly apparent, as is the need to transcend ethnic particularisms if we are to bring about the full development of the personality of each individual as a human being and a member of a universal humanity.

The pre–eminence of the community, the importance of maintaining the collective identity, and the degree of attachment to the group of origin are themes which more or less disappeared from educational research and practice in the immediate post–war years. One reason was undoubtedly a reaction against the nationalist excesses and totalitarian ideologies which had prevailed in the preceding years and the desire to work for peace in a spirit of international understanding and tolerance between nations and peoples. These concerns led to the creation of UNESCO and the adoption of the universal declaration of human rights. The conviction that the progress of knowledge was the only possible antidote to prejudice, racism, totalitarianism and the manipulation of minds helped give education a priority role in political action.

This is in fact the origin of contemporary multicultural education programmes. However, it is interesting to see what happened in the next four decades: year after year the same declarations of principle and the same act of faith concerning the essential function of education in the construction of a peaceful world were repeated, but at the same time the meaning attributed to the terms gradually changed and different shades of meaning crept in until reference was once again being made to and use made of concepts (such as ethnicity, race, group of origin, cultural identity) which had practically been in quarantine for a long period[15]. This has led to contemporary instruments dealing with multicultural education in which the importance of the culture of origin, cultural identity, respect for community traditions and membership of a group have become a permanent reference. One sometimes has the impression that those using these terms do not clearly perceive their underlying educational, philosophic and political implications.

In theory, these two sides of multicultural education could be easily combined. In practice this is however not the case. The harmonious development of the personality and intellectual differences of all children in a climate of liberty which enables the maximum benefit to be drawn from the cultural environment while at the same time keeping it at a certain distance, is not easy to achieve. All educational institutions are in unstable equilibrium vis–à–vis the community, and move from positions which are highly critical to the opposite extreme of excessive subordination. Neither of these situations is satisfactory, but the right balance is difficult to find since it depends on the role accorded the school in social and cultural reproduction. LeVine and White[16], in their book dealing with the crucial role of cultural factors in the development of the individual, bring out the importance of this dilemma by referring to the theoretical scheme used by Dahrendorf to explain life chances. According to Dahrendorf[17] the life chances of an individual are the joint product of the options (choices) and ligatures (social attachments) made available by the social structures. The maximum range of opportunities for an individual is theoretically determined when these two structural factors are at equilibrium. According to Dahrendorf, the growth of education resulted not merely in an expansion of options, but also in strengthening of ligatures. In Western education, especially from the Enlightenment onwards, the growth of opportunity and greater choice for the individual have had the upper hand whereas the significance of ligatures has been underestimated both in theory and in practice. The development of education is effective, i.e. has the maximum possible effects, where it increases life chances and opportunities. However, this result, according to Dahrendorf, cannot be achieved if the links between each individual and the community are destroyed (individualism) or become oppressive (collectivism).

It is thus essential to give in–depth consideration to the role of social linkages in personal development and to the importance that education should give to the community and to the factors that determine it and the variables which strengthen or weaken it. It is now necessary to develop a theory explaining the influence of social linkages on the life chances of individuals and hence on the organisation of education. It is pointless to deplore the weight of these linkages or conversely to celebrate their importance, to exhalt or deplore individualism and independence, since the development of the individual has a basic need for both of them. Clarification of these issues is an essential step towards establishing multicultural education on a solid theoretical basis.

It is surprising that there is almost no epistemological analysis in the literature on multicultural education concerning the cognitive scope of school culture. Every culture includes a specific system of relationships between the individual and nature and between one individual and another. Each cultural system includes a specific perception of space and time that structures the organisation and classification of knowledge as well as those of the individual and collective memory. The interaction between the culture of a people and its practices in acquiring and transmitting knowledge is very strong. The organisation of formal teaching as given in schools and the concept of the school itself greatly depend on the cultural model, and on the importance and significance attached in each culture to knowledge and to the concept of knowledge itself. The organisation of formal teaching as given in schools and the concept of the school itself depend on the cultural model, on the importance and significance attached in each culture to knowledge, and on the actual representation of knowledge within a given society or community. For example, the concept of knowledge in the Moslem culture or in the traditional Japanese culture is quite different from the concept of knowledge produced by Western cultures in the Enlightenment. Thus each culture influences in its own way the organisation of experience and the formation of cognitive abilities and even generates its own teaching model. All these questions are included only incidentally in the texts which discuss the organisation and development of multicultural education — so much so that it could almost be assumed that cognitive problems are not perceived as essential or do not have priority in the debate on multicultural education.

The examination of the main trends in the multicultural education policies described previously brings out a number of common characteristics and problems. Three general factors emerge from the analysis:

  i) Multicultural problems are not confined to the sphere of competences of the education systems;

ii) Ambitions in education policies concerning interactions between different cultural groups can only be modest;

iii) Most multicultural education programmes are not supported by a solid and clear theoretical structure.

Competences of the education system and multicultural reality

What is known as multicultural reality is in fact a pattern of different cultures that overlap and influence one another. This multicultural reality should thus be seen as a pattern of influences rather than as an unrelated series of facts, objects and customs. Accordingly, it is difficult to grasp the situation: the factors involved can be described, but it is not possible to describe the interactions between them, as is very well expressed by the authors of the following passage:

"As anthropologists remind us, cultures are not just collections of facts, common memories or vocabularies. When these aspects of culture are taken out of their original content and then reassembled into packaged curricula, they are unlikely to provide the sense of belonging and self–esteem that come from a culturally intact community that enjoys the respect of other communities. Reduced to curricula in the hands of professional educators, they represent an ironic victory of dominant cultural forms."[18]

The major difficulty in implementing education programmes using culture as a subject matter (cultural courses) originates in the source of cultural practices: here we are confronted with the symbolic and the imaginary, with subjective beliefs and collective memory[19]. On one side, there is the logic of the imagination or subjective belief, as Max Weber says, which nourishes the impulses, passions and myths accumulated in culture and, on the other, there is the logic which permeates school culture as it exists in OECD societies[20]. In view of its specific nature and the logic governing it (in the Western model), schools (in the sense of compulsory schooling and not curricula) cannot grasp or pass on the substratum of cultural behaviour and beliefs. When they deal with cultures, they can only keep to the surface of things and are thus inevitably exposed to the risk of teaching folklore and therefore of distorting cultural values. This conclusion is disputed by experts on multicultural education who consider that schools are capable of communicating to pupils the intensity of feelings and beliefs which underlie cultural practices of ethnic groups: by means of direct experience, cultural events, simulation techniques and role playing, it would at least be possible to attain a level of discreet understanding of cultural behaviour. The question remains whether ordinary teachers and schools are equipped to organise this type of exploration of cultural material and whether they have the time and skills necessary for the purpose.

It is understandable why education authorities dealing with ethnic minority groups hesitate when faced with the danger, clearly or less clearly perceived, of provoking reactions which are unpredictable and difficult to control since they are based on irrational and emotional considerations, an aspect of reality which has to be approached with the greatest caution. The danger is like that of playing with fire: anything can happen. Bratt Paulston quotes an example that illustrates the misunderstandings (and tensions) that can arise despite the good intentions: the way in which the Swedes reacted towards gypsies after they persisted in not sending their children to school, despite the liberal spirit of the new Swedish policy in favour of minorities. The Swedes had not imagined, said Bratt Paulston, that the principle of freedom of choice, which is a cornerstone of their policy, could be interpreted by the gipsies to mean that they could even refuse schooling. They had been given many options, but not this one. It was self—evident to the Swedes that the children had at least to go to school. The misunderstanding on this point was total: we continually attribute our own values to others[21].

Despite these difficulties and problems none of the OECD countries have hesitated in working out multicultural educational programmes with roughly the same objectives, i.e. to neutralise or prevent cultural conflicts, improve mutual understanding between different communities, and find out more about other people's culture. This being so, we are bound to ask what this trend signifies and particularly whether such objectives do not exceed the possibilities of the education system.

How can schools respond to the popular beliefs and imagination which nourish and form the core of all culture? Educators are divided in this respect: some are enthusiastic and do not hesitate to get involved and to arrange absorbing and exciting activities for their pupils, while others (the majority) remain cautious and are not sure what they should do. The role of the school in this area of intercultural relations should be to define its own place in rational and critical terms, in line with its principal *raison d'être*.

The present phase in the development of multicultural education is interesting because it marks a change in the way schools have dealt with cultural and linguistic differences. Traditionally, the educational approach to understanding ethnic groups and minority cultures has been to use stereotypes (partly produced, moreover, by the schools themselves), which enabled ethnic minority groups to be graded within a rational classification system in relation to a dominant group whose culture provided the co—ordinates for identifying differences and putting them in order. Thus the knowledge concerning minority group cultures passed on by schools was, however, much more significant: the value of this material was not in the objective information it gave on ethnic minorities or minority cultures, but rather in the fact that it showed the schools' view of these cultures.

This way of dealing with cultural material in schools is characteristic of the rationalist approach which implies the use of a specific method of observation and hence of acquisition of knowledge, and includes for example the invention of the cultural object. This type of teaching has been criticized with the spread of a new learning model based on experience and practice. Here, knowledge of cultural differences is no longer solely intellectual and abstract. Children come into direct contact with other cultures, find solutions to cultural conflicts, modify their reactions, discover their prejudices and explore their emotions vis—à—vis those with other values and another sensibility, and who express their emotions in a different way. Schools in which pupils from different ethnic groups meet provide a host of opportunities for multicultural education (and here the word *education* should be taken in its widest sense), for at these schools it is possible to obtain experience of socialisation in a multicultural environment, i.e. acquire forms of sociability making it possible to work, talk and exchange views with those from a different cultural background.

In order not to leave the development of children's multicultural experience to chance encounters, we can even go further by simulating (via role playing based on group dynamics) meetings with people belonging to other cultures. Teaching strategies and techniques are already available which give pupils the opportunity systematically to explore "standard" situations, to exercise their judgement in a methodical way (which reveals how the mechanics of judgement work), to elucidate the values they encounter and discover, and to test and try out principles underlying different beliefs. Some maintain that these techniques can be used in schools and that now is the right time for them; others are critical of this subjectivist and more or less therapeutic trend in education.

These methods propose a quite different kind of knowledge of cultural differences: many contemporary multicultural education programmes use them to replace the indirect formal knowledge offered by traditional–type teaching by direct knowledge gained not only from intellectual effort but also and more especially from practical and emotional experience. Textually transmitted knowledge is replaced by contextually acquired knowledge. This represents a radical change in the pedagogy.

The recent developments in multicultural education are associated with the ethnic revival, but also with the spread of new learning strategies that are no longer geared to formal teaching. The discussions and experiments under way, the search for new solutions or alternative systems of multicultural education are in a transitional phase between a declining teaching practice and another emerging: one outdated pedagogy about cultural differences is being replaced by a new, more functional method with new teaching objectives that have been developing for some years now in all OECD countries.

Despite the importance of the debate on multicultural education, it should be noted that initiatives, experiments and programmes concerning multicultural education have a marginal place in educational curricula and policies, with the possible exception of a few countries, particularly Australia and Canada. In Canada several teachers' organisations have multicultural education policies or anti–discrimination policies. In the province of Ontario the Minister of Education is drawing up a policy on race relations in education. However, most education systems are monocultural and monolingual (this fact is not in any way affected by the development of foreign language teaching).

In Canada, despite the relevance of multicultural education, it has been stated that "bilingual or multilingual education" — which are variants of multicultural education — "occurs only in very few classrooms, in very few schools, in only some language communities, and in only some provinces"[22]. In the United States, another country where ethnic problems are well known and where the debate on the assimilation of minority groups within the English–speaking melting pot has always been heated, the development of bilingual educational programmes continues to be opposed by a wide section of the public and the political world[23]. In 1983, only 10 per cent of children entitled to bilingual teaching actually received it. In Australia, another country where the range of cultures and languages is very wide, the development of multicultural education is recent and has not yet really modified the traditional approaches to teaching.

Everywhere multicultural education on a wide scale is practically non–existent, or is in an embryonic phase, as in the European countries. Although they show that education systems are being opened up along multicultural lines, educational programmes for immigrants' children concern only a small proportion of them (the percentage varies with the country from 20 to 70 per cent). On the other hand, it is difficult to quantify the number of programmes, courses, and initiatives concerning multiculturalism that are intended for the majority of pupils. Bilingual classes, which are another special application of multicultural education, are exceptional, for they exist only in specific regions, such as Yugoslavia, where special linguistic situations arise, in Catalonia and in the romansch valleys of the Grisons in Switzerland. In all cases, bilingual teaching is strictly territorial.

In practice, therefore, multicultural education, in the strict and in the broad sense of the term, is confined to the interstices of the system. A great deal is spoken about it, but the scale of the debate is not matched by the extent of the programmes. This again shows the enormous weight of the resistance, strong feelings and conflicting interests to be found within highly bureaucratic education systems.

The limits to multicultural education policies

Previous solutions used by teaching systems to deal with problems caused by cultural heterogeneity may be classified on the basis of two different strategies: a non–interventionist strategy whereby ethnic problems are settled by the free play of interactions between communities; and an interventionist policy based on the conviction that action by the authorities is necessary to attenuate any risk of social violence and injustice. For example, it has been said that UK policy is more in line with the former[24] and Swedish policy more with the latter.

All the policies of the various countries fall between these two positions. We will not discuss here the advantages and disadvantages of each option, for no criteria are available to assess which of the two strategies gives better results. There are probably no definite answers to such a question. The results depend greatly on local traditions, the administrative context, political style and the history of relations between ethnic minority communities and the majority. Solutions which have given satisfactory results in certain national situations, i.e. which have actually improved the school performance of children from ethnic minority groups or have helped children to adapt better to multicultural contexts, do not necessarily have the same results even when applied to another region of the same country. So far no country has found the right way of attenuating or correcting failures and shortcomings in the educational results of pupils from ethnic minority groups to any appreciable extent. This situation could be put down to a lack of multicultural education programmes or the poor quality of courses, which would suggest that to obtain uniform results and reduce failure, it would be sufficient to make more courses of better quality available. By analogy with what has already happened in other circumstances, it is doubtful that the average educational achievements of pupils belonging to ethnic minority groups can be improved simply by expanding multicultural education facilities, since it is known that these results do not depend solely on educational variables[25].

The main obstacle to overcome is the discrepancy between the nature of the problem and the solutions which are envisaged or feasible. Cultural or social remedies are proposed as an answer to a political and social question (the harmony of relationships between different communities and the inequality of opportunity affecting children in ethnic minority groups). Appropriate political action is vital for the social and political objectives of cultural and linguistic pluralism. When the junction between educational policy and social policy is not made or is not made properly, the treatment of cultural problems in schools is reduced, as has been observed in many cases, to a matter of folklore. As there is no right way of treating problems, the answer is finally to go in for culturalism, i.e. to build up, propose and display fictitious identities consisting of remnants of collective cultures[26].

The advantage of the folklore approach is that it gives the impression of treating multicultural problems simply because interest is expressed in minority cultures. However, it does not challenge the order of hierarchical importance in which the cultures within a given society are classified, nor does it question the balance of strength between cultures and between communities. The fragments of popular traditions presented at the multicultural events organised at schools, the examples of domestic objects shown to pupils, and the costumes put on during picturesque ceremonies divorced from their historical context are simply museum pieces that have lost their practical justification. "They are artefacts that do not refer back to the codes, knowledge and types of ability which, in a culture, make it possible to think out and see the world in perspective ... behind the picturesque effect, it means that cultural identity is relegated to the timelessness of roots and that culture is thereby dissociated from history"[27], and from policy. Nevertheless, the advocates of multicultural education, while accepting the limits of the folklore approach, point out, without in any way approving it, that it is not as bad as is claimed since it can take the first steps towards a more open approach and towards a more profound understanding of other cultures and of ways of thinking different to one's own.

Multicultural education easily lapses into moralism and folklore if all aspects of the socio-economic situation of ethnic minority groups are not taken into account. But is also difficult to provide multicultural education for an epistemologic or even philosophical reason. The criticism of ethnocentrism, the struggle against the remnants of cultural imperialism in education programmes, the suspension of all value judgement in the name of the equivalence of cultures, and cultural relativism, have all had a far-reaching influence on the climate of education and teaching. To realise this it is enough to look at the changes in history and geography curricula over the past decades. There are both good and less good aspects to this development and this is not the place for their assessment. One point is nevertheless important: the doubt sown among teachers as to the epistemological value of rational thought and scientific knowledge. The revision and criticism of curricula under the influence of doctrines and schools of thought inspired by the Declaration of Human Rights and the decolonisation debate have shaken some very well established aspects of the school education, by denouncing the ethnocentric content of certain courses, the prejudices transmitted by schools, the open or concealed racial discrimination found in them and the representation of knowledge that they offer.

This condemnation of ethnocentrism has sometimes been seen as an attack on rationalism and rationality which underlie the Western educational tradition and scientific knowledge. It is possible to imagine educational models based on other ways of thinking and organised by reference to other forms of knowledge. However, it is difficult for the time being to envisage a change to the educational model predominant in the OECD countries. It is likely that for these countries in the future the school will continue to be acknowledged and supported as the home of rational knowledge, the place where we learn to think rationally and logically. The consequence for multicultural education seems to be that it will become established in schools all the more easily to the extent that it ties in with the logic of the cognitive process which takes place there. As stated by one of the contributors to the recent monograph on immigration brought out by the French publication *Esprit*, "the intercultural aspect cannot be divorced, in schools, from teaching objectives, unless it is to become insignificant or be rejected; an 'open' culture that can be modified ad infinitum as new communities meet is, and can be, no more than a process of increasing the depth and scope of our own culture"[28].

To get some idea of what should be done, reference must be made to the basic function of teaching. Education cannot solve problems where cultural and linguistic issues are at stake; what it can and must do, on the contrary, is promote rational understanding of conflict, tensions, and the processes involved, provoke a critical awareness of cultural interactions, and provide a basis for the analysis of concepts that will prevent obscurantist, chauvinist and irrationalist explanations from being accepted. School is above all — or at least should be — the place of rational knowledge: its primary task is thus to provide information, explain and analyse problems and subject them to criticism.

Weaknesses of the theoretical framework

Observation of multicultural education policies does not make it possible to formulate valid suggestions to help draw up convincing multicultural education programmes and policies, although the mass of work on multicultural education experience and what has been done so far do point to much better things for the future. Cummins[29], for example, maintains that it is already possible to propose a scientifically valid theory of bilingual education. Churchill has made the first and so far only classification of multicultural education programmes in the OECD countries based on objectives pursued and putting programmes in three categories[30]:

— Assimilationist programmes, in which the more or less explicit aim is to adapt minorities to the majority culture;
— Remedial programmes, designed to eliminate flagrant discrimination and prejudices in regard to minorities in schools, curricula and textbooks;
— Egalitarian programmes, which fully recognise the existence of minority cultures which are given equal rights with the majority.

In practice these distinctions are much less marked, as shown by the American and UK programmes.

In the *United States*, the indecision and vagueness of American policy with regard to bilingual education is universally recognised. Even today, over 15 years after the passing of the Bilingual Education Act of 1968, neither agreement nor consensus has been reached on the goals of bilingual education. Despite the rulings of the Supreme Court in many actions arising from the Act, the initial vagueness has not yet disappeared, as proved by the following comments from the *Harvard Encyclopedia of American Ethnic Groups*:

"The Bilingual Education Act, like most congressional legislation, was passed in response to the demands of diverse interest groups and was, of necessity, sufficiently vaguely worded to satisfy advocates with conflicting views. It had no commonly agreed–on purpose. At a minimum it aimed to use the native tongue of un–English–speaking children for a limited number of years in order to ensure the acquisition of basic skills such as arithmetic and writing. At the maximum its goal was not only the provision of temporary help to children in the process of linguistic assimilation, but also linguistic and cultural maintenance — the preservation of the language and values of a foreign culture."

In the *United Kingdom*, English and Welsh policy with regard to the educational problems of the minorities seemed to be not quite clear and consistent either. Until the publication of the *Swann Report* in 1985, so many delays and changes in course have occurred that McLean[31] even claims that UK policy in this field is simply a patchwork of various solutions adopted under the pressure of events (for example, the riots in the black districts of major towns) or imposed by the requirement to adapt UK legislation to international conventions or EEC directives. However, Kirp[32] disagrees with such an interpretation. He considers that one of the greater merits of UK policy compared with that of the United States is precisely that, from the start, it adopted a low profile and a pragmatic approach, which may give an impression of inconsistency because of the vagueness of objectives, but which are effective since they enable action to be adapted to different circumstances.

Hesitation or inconsistency is the common lot of all multicultural education policies. There is no reason to be shocked about it, since it is due to the extreme complexity of multicultural objectives in which political, linguistic, cultural and psycho–pedagogical questions overlap. Technical solutions — for example, the revision of curricula, the production of textbooks, the adjustment of timetables and the introduction of special courses or new options, which to many educators at least have the merit of appearing practical — often prove ineffective when they are proposed or adopted without an analysis of their relevance to the problems involved. The uncertainty, the contradictions, the lack of continuity, the backtracking or simply the caution encountered whenever the trend of multicultural education policies is examined are inevitable. This is all the more so to the extent that educational bureaucracy by its very nature tends to aggravate rather than counteract them.

The development of multicultural education programmes is not only hampered by administrative difficulties or political hesitation. There is another more insidious obstacle, a psychological one and hence more difficult to detect. The opening of a frank and open dialogue between majority and minority leaders would itself constitute a victory, since to reach that point it may be necessary to overcome mistrust, suspicion or doubt as to the other side's motives. Churchill, who is an observer sympathetic to the minority cause, notes this situation with a certain bitterness:

"For these persons involved in trying to respond to minority needs in an open, fair–minded manner, a serious psychological effort is required to set aside many of their own deeply–held values concerning the importance of having one language and one culture embedded in an educational system; once they have made this effort and accepted multicultural education as a solution to current problems, they feel somehow deceived to discover that putting it into practice may not end all problems and will not eliminate further demands from minorities for additional recognition."[33]

It must not be forgotten that ethnic community leaders are not faced solely by a cultural or humanitarian problem which could be overcome with a little goodwill and determination. What is at stake for them, as it is for the representatives of the dominant group, is political, and relates essentially to the sharing of power and to relative economic strength. To reach solutions satisfactory to both sides and acceptable to all the parties concerned, recriminations and fears have to be brought to the surface, more explicit approaches adopted and an attempt made not to be influenced by what is simply implicit, the aim being to create the most favourable basis for a discussion unfettered by prejudice. The effectiveness of multicultural education can only be judged in the long term.

NOTES AND REFERENCES

1. Idea expressed by Kowalczewski, P.: "Race and Education. Racism, Diversity and Inequality. Implications for Multicultural Education", in *Oxford Review of Education*, Vol. 8, No. 2, 1982. The fear of a split in the local community was very marked in the United Kingdom in 1984 when the Bradford town council was discussing the sale of three *i)* local authority schools to the Moslem community (see for example Gross, J.: "When in Bradford ...", in *Times Educational Supplement*, 25.5.1984; Selbourne, D.: "The Culture Clash in Bradford", in *New Society*, 26.4.1984).

2. Epstein, N.: *Language, Ethnicity and the Schools*, University Press, Washington, 1977.

3. Glazer, N.: "Cultural Differences and Equality of Educational Achievement", in *Multicultural Education*, OECD/CERI, Paris, 1987.

4. Cohen, G.: "The Politics of Bilingual Education", in *Oxford Review of Education*, Vol. 10, No. 2, 1984.

5. Fleming, J.: "Heritage Languages and the Policy of Multiculturalism", in Cummins, J.: *Heritage Language Education: Issues and Directions*. Proceedings of the Saskatoon Conference, June 1981. Ministry of Supply, Ottawa, 1983.

6. De Certeau, M.: "The Management of Ethnic Resources: Schooling for Diversity", in *Multicultural Education*, OECD/CERI, *op. cit.*

7. Noted by Cummins, J, *op. cit.*

8. Roberts, L.W., Clifton, K.A.: "Exploring the Ideology of Canadian Multiculturalism", in *Canadian Public Policy*, Vol. VIII, Winter 1982.

9. De Certeau, M., *op. cit.*

10. Kowalczewski, P.S., *op. cit.*

11. Porcher, L.: *The Education of the Children of Migrant Workers in Europe. Interculturalism and Teacher Training.* Council for Cultural Co-operation. Council of Europe, Strasbourg, 1981.

12. Boos Nünning, U., Hohmann, M., Reich, H. and Witteck, F.: *Aufnahmeunterricht, Muttersprachlicher Unterricht, Interkultureller Unterricht.* Publikation Alpha, Oldenburg, München, 1983.

13. *Immigrants' Children at School*, OECD/CERI, Paris, 1987.

14. Smolicz, J.J.: "Is the Monolingual Nation-State out-of-date? A comparative study of language policies in Australia and the Philippines", in *Comparative Education*, Vol. 20, No. 2, 1984.

15. This trend is very well analysed by Finkelkrant, A.: *La défaite de la pensée*, Gallimard, Paris, 1987.

16. LeVine, R.A., White, M.J.: Human Conditions. *The Cultural Basis of Educational Developments*, Routledge & Kegan Paul, New York, 1986.

17. Dahrendorf, R.: *Life Chances*. University of Chicago Press. Chicago, 1978. Mentioned by LeVine (*op. cit.*).

18. Olneck, M.: Lazerson, M.: "Education", in *Harvard Encyclopedia of American Ethnic Groups*. Harvard University Press, Cambridge, 1980.

19. The definition of the ethnic group given by Max Weber takes into account this irrational, almost mysterious aspect of its existence: the ethnic groups are "these human groups which have a *subjective belief* in a parent community based on similarities of behaviour or customs, or both, or on memories of colonisation or migration, so that this *belief* becomes important for the *spread* of communication — whether a community of race objectively exists or not" (our emphasis). Max Weber, *Economie et Société*. French version published by Plon, Paris, 1971, p. 416.

20. In his contribution to the CERI project on multicultural education, Michel de Certeau (*op. cit.*) contrasts the individual rights, which constitute modern western societies and have given rise to the concept of equality and individual justice, with the old collective rights whereby the *group* was recognised as having priority over its members. Individual rights comply with factual logic: measurements, comparisons and judgements are made; collective rights are in the realm of the imaginary: collective expressions — family, household and clan — govern cultural as well as economic relations between the members of the group, according to a non–formal logic of equality.

21. Bratt Paulston, C.: *op. cit.*

22. Cummins, J.: *op. cit.*

23. Glazer, N.: *op. cit.* The movement for adopting English as the official language of the United States is very significant. For the moment, 13 states have already approved a bill in this sense. Following bilingual education activists these bills can affect not only the development of bilingual education in the United States but all the bilingual public services as well.

24. Kirp, D.L.: "Doing Good by Doing Little", in *Race and Schooling in Britain*. University of California Press, 1979.

25. In this respect the findings of the Swann Committee in the United Kingdom on the education of children from ethnic minority groups are extremely instructive: (*Education for All*. Report of the Committee of Inquiry into the Education of Children from Ethnic Minority Groups. Secretary of State for Education and Science. HMSO, London, 1985.)

26. Gokalp, A.: "Identités, altérités", in *Ecole et socialisme*, No. 30, June 1984.

27. Gokalp, A.: *op. cit.*

28. Pierrot, A.: "L'école française et ses étrangers", in *Esprit*, No. 102, June 1985.

    A clear analysis of the importance of the rationalist tradition and logical/deductive thought, which is also an instructive criticism of the influence of cultural relativism and irrationalism in the discussion on education — these are major themes underlying the intercultural positions and multicultural approaches appealing for the respect of cultural identities — is given in the latest works by Bouveresse, B.: *Le philosophe chez les autophages*, Minuit, Paris, 1984; *Rationalité et cynisme*, Minuit, Paris, 1985.

29. Cummins, J.: *op. cit.*

30. Churchill, S.: *The Education of Linguistic and Cultural Minorities in the OECD Countries*. Multilingual Matters, Clevedon, 1986.

31. McLean, M.: "Education and Cultural Diversity in Britain. Recent Immigrant Groups", in *Comparative Education*, Vol. 19, No. 2, 1983.

32. Kirp, D.: *op. cit.*

33. Churchill, S.: "Policy Development for Education in Multicultural Societies. Trends and Processes in the OECD Countries", in *Multicultural Education*, OECD/CERI, *op. cit.*

Chapter V

CONCLUSIONS

In the preceding pages the importance of political issues in multicultural education has been repeatedly stressed. This aspect will not be dealt with in these conclusions which will address the educational problems alone. Throughout the analysis observations have been made concerning multicultural education policies. These observations will now be looked at as a whole to see what general lessons can be learnt about the way in which multicultural education programmes are developing.

Our approach is based on two salient facts:

i)   Children not belonging to majority groups are as a rule (though with exceptions) disadvantaged in educational terms, have below average school results, and hence less opportunities than other children;

ii) Most corrective steps taken in schools fail to come up to expectations: many multicultural education programmes have proved relatively ineffective.

A number of distinct pointers that could guide the future development of multicultural education stand out clearly:

i)   The development of multicultural education forms part of a deep–seated change in educational thinking resulting from the criticism of traditional teaching methods and the traditional concept of learning based on formalist cognitive theory. The spread of multicultural education is linked to modern educational thought derived from cognitive theories of behaviourist and naturalist origin;

ii)   The systematic reference in documents dealing with multicultural education to community values, the importance of cultural identity, to links with the group of origin, to the need for respect for traditions and customs, and to the role played by attachment and loyalty to groups of origin in the development of the personality ... all point to a renewal of interest in the community aspect of education. The function and very existence of this have been played down by teaching which, since the end of World War II, has been based on the development of the individual, respect for individual freedom of choice and on training for autonomy and independence. The advent of multicultural education signifies a renewed regard for the community and the end of a certain guise of individualism;

iii) Situated as they are at the meeting point of conflicting educational postulates (individualism or collectivism) and of teaching methods which are also in conflict (spontaneity or artificiality), multicultural education programmes cannot be successfully implanted within education systems without in–depth consideration of the cognitive function of the school and of the mental processes involved in the transmission of culture within the school;

iv) Human rights are an obligatory reference for multicultural education which is borne along by the current of ideas and initiatives inspired by the enlightened and humanist political theory of the immediate post–war period. The best guarantee against the excesses of cultural relativism ought to be human rights, respect for which constitutes an inviolable limit for any open cultural policy;

v) Multicultural education programmes should concern all children — not solely those outside the culturally and linguistically dominant groups. Restricted multicultural education designed for special categories of children (of migrants or ethnic minorities) can be less successful and can be attacked by virtue of its compensatory and welfare character.

Since the school cannot act upon the non–educational variables to improve the schooling of children from ethnic minority groups, we must identify the educational variables that affect the provision of education and try to change them to obtain better results. However, facile illusions must be avoided[1] since we know that the effect of these variables on children's performance is slight[2].

Starting from these considerations, we reach the following conclusions:

i) It is not logical to propose multicultural education programmes if the schools are not good, that is to say if the quality of education is poor. The first aim of an education policy for minority ethnic groups must be to improve the quality of education; when quality is insufficient, children from poor social classes and in particular children from minority ethnic groups (for instance, Blacks or Hispanics in the United States) suffer more than the others, for it is hard for them to recoup, outside school, what they fail to learn in school. The poor quality of a number of schools with concentrations of children from minority ethnic groups is one of the main reasons for the high rate of educational failure.

In this connection it is essential to improve linguistic education considerably in order to enhance skills in oral and written communication using the school language. Accordingly, schools should first aim at successful teaching of the language of instruction, which is often the country's official language or its equivalent (English in the United States, for example), a knowledge of which is essential both for subsequent schooling and for proper vocational training. The debate concerning bilingual teaching models should not be allowed to obscure this objective. Teaching the native language is warranted when it helps to improve chances of success among children who do not speak the language of instruction very well. This has been proved correct[3] but does not mean that teaching of languages of origin is always effective. To be so, certain conditions that are now coming to be clearly identified by scientific research have to be met. We are now beginning to understand what must be done and what must be avoided to get decent results from the teaching of languages of origin or from bilingual education.

74

ii) There can be no good schools without good teachers: this is a basic truth of education. To improve the quality of schools with problems we need exceptionally competent teachers. No progress is possible in the education of the children of migrants or ethnic groups if teachers' recruitment is insufficient, if their qualifications are inadequate, and if there are no career incentives to attract the best teachers to the schools most in need — in other words, the ones attended by a majority of poor, migrant or coloured children. Nor is it possible to think of extending multicultural education programmes to all children unless all teachers are given solid theoretical instruction about the problems of interactions between different cultures, implying some study of philosophy, cultural anthropology, linguistics, educational sociology and the psychology of learning. It is not enough to show that bilingual education or L1 or L2 courses are sometimes effective; ordinary schools, and not only experimental or *avant-garde* ones, have to have the right equipment and resources. Indeed, a number of surveys in the United States, Sweden, Germany and Belgium on the qualifications of teachers giving courses in languages and cultures of origin or bilingual education show that a high percentage do not have the qualifications required or a sufficient knowledge of the language they are supposed to teach.

iii) In the current state of knowledge[4], we can assert that bilingual education may encourage the intellectual development of bilingual children and hence promote educational achievement. Yet this assertion does not mean that such instruction is necessary for success. This may be achieved without bilingual education or native language and culture programmes, as is the case, for instance, with a proportion of children of Asian origin in the United Kingdom and the United States. But it can be argued from several pieces of research that, when bilingual education or native language and culture programmes are of high quality, substantial benefit accrues to children because strengthening their knowledge of a language learnt naturally also "empowers" the children and enhances their learning capabilities.

Bilingual education and the teaching of heritage languages or languages of origin are important not only on educational grounds. There are also economic and commercial arguments in favour of language teaching and for substantial numbers of people being able to express themselves in several languages. An economy that wants to make itself felt at international level, maintain its position and conquer new markets is in need of this kind of asset. Obviously it is more economic to maintain and exploit the existing linguistic capital of a country by helping children to retain or improve the language they speak at home or which is spoken around them (the level of knowledge of the domestic language is unimportant, what counts is to start from what knowledge there is) than to build up this capital from nothing. Likewise, it would be desirable to prevent such capital from being destroyed or disappearing. This is only logical; unfortunately in politics logic is not the only thing that counts, as is only too apparent in the way language teaching is organised.

In all probability courses in languages and cultures of origin and bilingual education were introduced for symbolic rather than economic reasons. Allowing children to study the language spoken in the home or to use that language where it was not the language of the school was a concession to cultural or political pressures (the need for a broad general culture, respect for family traditions, maintenance of heritage languages, resistance — in principle — to assimilation, keeping at a distance from other ethnic communities or keeping open the possibility of returning to the country of origin) rather than a choice made in application of a policy concerned with the foreign language skills of the national community.

iv) The school is an institution that produces, organises, administers and distributes a particular product that may be termed educational culture, made up of a body of knowledge organised according to given criteria, which is taught and assimilated by specific memorisation procedures and transmitted by means of clearly defined linguistic codes. In transmitting a certain type of knowledge in sequences organised on the basis of logical criteria, the school has a far-reaching effect on thought processes and representations (the *forma mentis* or "frame of mind") involved in the acquisition of rational knowledge. The institution of the school as it has developed in the Western world is both the outcome of a rationalist cultural tradition and the place where that tradition is reproduced and celebrated.

In this connection, the organisation of multicultural education with the introduction of native language and culture courses into the curriculum raises a specific cognitive problem. The extension of multicultural education is more than the mere updating of education programmes by including fresh knowledge or even new disciplines. To varying degrees it gives access to other forms of knowledge and to other cultural traditions with knowledge different in content and internal structure from that of the school tradition. The cognitive aspect of multicultural education programmes should not be underestimated since it is of considerable epistemological significance. The way in which multicultural education fits into education systems is a delicate matter since it touches on a sensitive point of the teaching process, i.e. the forms and ranking of knowledge. Educational activism, human rights, the problems of teachers or political pressures should not be used as excuses for avoiding thorough investigation of this issue.

v) Neither should we overlook the fact that the development of multicultural education is connected with the educational development of equal opportunity policies. The introduction of increasingly elaborate multicultural education programmes in most OECD countries from the 1970s onwards was helped by the new atmosphere created by equal opportunity policies. Condemnation of blatant discrimination against immigrant children and minority ethnic groups in schools strengthened the criticism of monolingual and monocultural education systems by human and civil rights groups and encouraged the spread of multicultural education.

Of course it did not take equal opportunity policies to reveal the extent of the underachievement and school failure of minority children. Studies of educational inequality revealed nothing that the minorities did not know already. They were well aware of the problems of their children at school since they were directly involved. What is new is the explanation now given of this situation: underachievement by these children is no longer seen as a special case, the consequence of so–called cultural backwardness or socio–cultural handicap, but as the effect of educational strategies unadapted to the logic governing the way in which education functions. Since efforts to resolve the educational difficulties of minority children were thus no longer the concern of the minorities alone, they acquired new political significance and could be carried forward with support from other quarters.

The factor which changed the thrust of minorities' demands in regard to education by emphasizing the struggle against educational inequality was, according to Hutmacher[5], the emergence of a new paradigm to explain underachievement, whereby it was no longer inevitable, as had been the case with the biological explanation, nor the result of class, as followed from the sociological explanation, but was due to cultural variables (in the 1970s there was a lot of talk about socio–cultural handicaps). This explanation opens the way to new educational remedies since the abolition of inequality in school is no longer beyond the capabilities of the schools themselves. Educational action to deal with underachievement thus becomes a possibility. The first result of this change has been the introduction of compensatory education and positive discrimination programmes. Many multicultural education programmes have been influenced by this theory. But the results of these programmes (educational inequality has not been reduced and the gap between the average performance of majority and minority children is still considerable) have cast doubt on the effectiveness of this approach and hence on the validity of the underlying theory. The theory must be revised if multicultural education is to have any prospect of developing in the future.

vi) Present circumstances are both favourable and unfavourable to the development of multicultural education. The structural transformation of the economy now under way is producing ever greater interdependence among national economies. Countries are having to show initiative, drive and inventiveness to keep up with increasingly fierce international competition. This can only be done by staying ahead in the technological and scientific race, promoting scientific training and research and making the best use of a country's human resources. Parameters relevant to the preparation of education policies to meet the demands of the economies of the 1980s thus have to meet two requirements: to raise the level of skills of the population so as to favour continuous growth of sectors of the economy with a high degree of technological and scientific innovation; and keep as many children as possible in secondary education by reducing losses due to school failure.

On the first point, the main consequence for education will be the increased importance of scientific disciplines in curricula so as to improve and strengthen children's scientific background. The unity of science and the universality of scientific thought are two decisive factors for growth, which explains the growing importance of scientific content in education. On the second point, the objective can only be attained if the ways in which education systems are organised and run become more flexible and differentiated, by modifying the structure and content of courses to make the most of the cultural and linguistic particularisms which are another vigorous element of growth. In the same way, more resources have to go to schools where children of migrants and ethnic groups are concentrated and which are often in underprivileged areas and badly equipped[6]. It is by no means certain that this would improve the performance of such children, but it would at least make it possible to give them a better reception and make them feel at home in school. It is difficult to say what the results of this type of schooling might be but they could be no worse than those being achieved at present.

One last factor favouring the development of multicultural education should be mentioned: the concern of political leaders in most OECD countries to avoid social unrest and maintain a minimum social consensus around a few basic concepts which serve to hold society together. In contemporary multicultural societies it is not easy to do this, to avoid exacerbating racial tension, excessive nationalism or inter-community violence. The inequality and discrimination found in these complex societies, the social costs of structural adjustment, violations of human rights, obstacles to communication and civil rights problems all stand in the way of social integration. Policies to maintain or encourage harmonious coexistence of different ethnic groups have to be drawn up extremely carefully and implemented with great skill and subtlety. Multicultural education programmes are one aspect of these policies and if well conceived[7] could contribute to their success.

However, it would be wrong to be too ambitious. The introduction of multicultural education remains problematic for reasons which have frequently been explained. Its inclusion in curricula runs up against a well-established educational tradition which in OECD countries has produced prestigious forms of instruction along with educational practices marked by the spirit of nationalism. It is to be feared that, in spite of the validity of the principle of schooling adapted to cultural and linguistic pluralism, multicultural education programmes will in practice remain dominated by educational and cultural traditions sufficiently resistant to keep them in subjection.

NOTES AND REFERENCES

1. The Swann Report (*Education for All*. Report of the Committee of Inquiry into the Education of Children from Ethnic Minority Groups. HMSO, London, March 1985) contains very careful analysis of this aspect of the inequality of educational opportunities.

2. See in this connection the classic study on inequality in education by Jencks, C.: *Inequalities: A Reassessment of the Effect of Family and Schooling in America*. Basic Books, New York, 1972.

3. Cummins, J.: "Theory and Policy in Bilingual Education", in *Multicultural Education*, OECD/CERI, Paris, 1987.

4. *Ibid.*

5. Hutmacher, W.: "Cultural Issues in Educational Policies: A Retrospect", in *Multicultural Education*, OECD/CERI, *op. cit.*

6. OECD, "Structural Adjustment and Economic Performance. Synthesis Report". OECD, Paris, 1987.

7. Smolicz distinguishes between divisive cultural factors (religion, politics) and unifying cultural factors (language, gastronomy, celebrations, etc.). In the process of acculturation, language for example has a different effect from religion: it is possible to be bilingual (a cultural enrichment) but not "bi–religious" (from the standpoint of belief, of course) (Smolicz, J.: "Multiculturalism and an Overarching Framework of Values: Some educational responses for ethnically plural societies", in *European Journal for Education*, Vol. 19, No. 1, 1984.

WHERE TO OBTAIN OECD PUBLICATIONS
OÙ OBTENIR LES PUBLICATIONS DE L'OCDE

ARGENTINA - ARGENTINE
Carlos Hirsch S.R.L.,
Florida 165, 4° Piso,
(Galeria Guemes) 1333 Buenos Aires
Tel. 33.1787.2391 y 30.7122

AUSTRALIA - AUSTRALIE
D.A. Book (Aust.) Pty. Ltd.
11-13 Station Street (P.O. Box 163)
Mitcham, Vic. 3132   Tel. (03) 873 4411

AUSTRIA - AUTRICHE
OECD Publications and Information Centre,
4 Simrockstrasse,
5300 Bonn (Germany)   Tel. (0228) 21.60.45
Gerold & Co., Graben 31, Wien 1 Tel. 52.22.35

BELGIUM - BELGIQUE
Jean de Lannoy,
Avenue du Roi 202
B-1060 Bruxelles   Tel. (02) 538.51.69

CANADA
Renouf Publishing Company Ltd
1294 Algoma Road, Ottawa, Ont. K1B 3W8
Tel. (613) 741-4333
Stores:
61 rue Sparks St., Ottawa, Ont. K1P 5R1
Tel. (613) 238-8985
211 rue Yonge St., Toronto, Ont. M5B 1M4
Tel: (416) 363-3171
Federal Publications Inc.,
301-303 King St. W.,
Toronto, Ont. M5V 1J5   Tel. (416)581-1552
Les Éditions la Liberté inc.,
3020 Chemin Sainte-Foy,
Sainte-Foy, P.Q. G1X 3V6, Tel. (418)658-3763

DENMARK - DANEMARK
Munksgaard Export and Subscription Service
35, Nørre Søgade, DK-1370 København K
Tel. +45.1.12.85.70

FINLAND - FINLANDE
Akateeminen Kirjakauppa,
Keskuskatu 1, 00100 Helsinki 10 Tel. 0.12141

FRANCE
OCDE/OECD
Mail Orders/Commandes par correspondance :
2, rue André-Pascal,
75775 Paris Cedex 16   Tel. (1) 45.24.82.00
Bookshop/Librairie : 33, rue Octave-Feuillet
75016 Paris
Tel. (1) 45.24.81.67 or/ou (1) 45.24.81.81
Librairie de l'Université,
12a, rue Nazareth,
13602 Aix-en-Provence   Tel. 42.26.18.08

GERMANY - ALLEMAGNE
OECD Publications and Information Centre,
4 Simrockstrasse,
5300 Bonn   Tel. (0228) 21.60.45

GREECE - GRÈCE
Librairie Kauffmann,
28, rue du Stade, 105 64 Athens Tel. 322.21.60

HONG KONG
Government Information Services,
Publications (Sales) Office,
Information Services Department
No. 1, Battery Path, Central

ICELAND - ISLANDE
Snæbjörn Jónsson & Co., h.f.,
Hafnarstræti 4 & 9,
P.O.B. 1131 – Reykjavik
Tel. 13133/14281/11936

INDIA - INDE
Oxford Book and Stationery Co.,
Scindia House, New Delhi 110001
Tel. 331.5896/5308
17 Park St., Calcutta 700016   Tel. 240832

INDONESIA - INDONÉSIE
Pdii-Lipi, P.O. Box 3065/JKT.Jakarta
Tel. 583467

IRELAND - IRLANDE
TDC Publishers - Library Suppliers,
12 North Frederick Street, Dublin 1
Tel. 744835-749677

ITALY - ITALIE
Libreria Commissionaria Sansoni,
Via Benedetto Fortini 120/10,
Casella Post. 552
50125 Firenze   Tel. 055/645415
Via Bartolini 29, 20155 Milano   Tel. 365083
La diffusione delle pubblicazioni OCSE viene
assicurata dalle principali librerie ed anche da :
Editrice e Libreria Herder,
Piazza Montecitorio 120, 00186 Roma
Tel. 6794628
Libreria Hœpli,
Via Hœpli 5, 20121 Milano Tel. 865446
Libreria Scientifica
Dott. Lucio de Biasio "Aeiou"
Via Meravigli 16, 20123 Milano Tel. 807679

JAPAN - JAPON
OECD Publications and Information Centre,
Landic Akasaka Bldg., 2-3-4 Akasaka,
Minato-ku, Tokyo 107   Tel. 586.2016

KOREA - CORÉE
Kyobo Book Centre Co. Ltd.
P.O.Box: Kwang Hwa Moon 1658,
Seoul   Tel. (REP) 730.78.91

LEBANON - LIBAN
Documenta Scientifica/Redico,
Edison Building, Bliss St.,
P.O.B. 5641, Beirut   Tel. 354429-344425

MALAYSIA/SINGAPORE -
MALAISIE/SINGAPOUR
University of Malaya Co-operative Bookshop
Ltd.,
7 Lrg 51A/227A, Petaling Jaya
Malaysia   Tel. 7565000/7565425
Information Publications Pte Ltd
Pei-Fu Industrial Building,
24 New Industrial Road No. 02-06
Singapore 1953   Tel. 2831786, 2831798

NETHERLANDS - PAYS-BAS
SDU Uitgeverij
Christoffel Plantijnstraat 2
Postbus 20014
2500 EA's-Gravenhage   Tel. 070-789911
Voor bestellingen: Tel. 070-789880

NEW ZEALAND - NOUVELLE-ZÉLANDE
Government Printing Office Bookshops:
Auckland: Retail Bookshop, 25 Rutland Stseet,
Mail Orders, 85 Beach Road
Private Bag C.P.O.
Hamilton: Retail: Ward Street,
Mail Orders, P.O. Box 857
Wellington: Retail, Mulgrave Street, (Head
Office)
Cubacade World Trade Centre,
Mail Orders, Private Bag
Christchurch: Retail, 159 Hereford Street,
Mail Orders, Private Bag
Dunedin: Retail, Princes Street,
Mail Orders, P.O. Box 1104

NORWAY - NORVÈGE
Narvesen Info Center – NIC,
Bertrand Narvesens vei 2,
P.O.B. 6125 Etterstad, 0602 Oslo 6
Tel. (02) 67.83.10, (02) 68.40.20

PAKISTAN
Mirza Book Agency
65 Shahrah Quaid-E-Azam, Lahore 3 Tel. 66839

PHILIPPINES
I.J. Sagun Enterprises, Inc.
P.O. Box 4322 CPO Manila
Tel. 695-1946, 922-9495

PORTUGAL
Livraria Portugal, Rua do Carmo 70-74,
1117 Lisboa Codex   Tel. 360582/3

SINGAPORE/MALAYSIA -
SINGAPOUR/MALAISIE
See "Malaysia/Singapor". Voir
« Malaisie/Singapour»

SPAIN - ESPAGNE
Mundi-Prensa Libros, S.A.,
Castelló 37, Apartado 1223, Madrid-28001
Tel. 431.33.99
Libreria Bosch, Ronda Universidad 11,
Barcelona 7   Tel. 317.53.08/317.53.58

SWEDEN - SUÈDE
AB CE Fritzes Kungl. Hovbokhandel,
Box 16356, S 103 27 STH,
Regeringsgatan 12,
DS Stockholm   Tel. (08) 23.89.00
Subscription Agency/Abonnements:
Wennergren-Williams AB,
Box 30004, S104 25 Stockholm Tel. (08)54.12.00

SWITZERLAND - SUISSE
OECD Publications and Information Centre,
4 Simrockstrasse,
5300 Bonn (Germany)   Tel. (0228) 21.60.45
Librairie Payot,
6 rue Grenus, 1211 Genève 11
Tel. (022) 31.89.50
Maditec S.A.
Ch. des Palettes 4
1020 – Renens/Lausanne Tel. (021) 635.08.65
United Nations Bookshop/Librairie des Nations-
Unies
Palais des Nations, 1211 – Geneva 10
Tel. 022-34-60-11 (ext. 48 72)

TAIWAN - FORMOSE
Good Faith Worldwide Int'l Co., Ltd.
9th floor, No. 118, Sec.2, Chung Hsiao E. Road
Taipei   Tel. 391.7396/391.7397

THAILAND - THAILANDE
Suksit Siam Co., Ltd., 1715 Rama IV Rd.,
Samyam Bangkok 5   Tel. 2511630
INDEX Book Promotion & Service Ltd.
59/6 Soi Lang Suan, Ploenchit Road
Patjumamwan, Bangkok 10500
Tel. 250-1919, 252-1066

TURKEY - TURQUIE
Kültur Yayinlari Is-Türk Ltd. Sti.
Atatürk Bulvari No: 191/Kat. 21
Kavaklidere/Ankara   Tel. 25.07.60
Dolmabahce Cad. No: 29
Besiktas/Istanbul   Tel. 160.71.88

UNITED KINGDOM - ROYAUME-UNI
H.M. Stationery Office,
Postal orders only: (01)873-8483
P.O.B. 276, London SW8 5DT
Telephone orders: (01) 873-9090, or
Personal callers:
49 High Holborn, London WC1V 6HB
Branches at: Belfast, Birmingham,
Bristol, Edinburgh, Manchester

UNITED STATES - ÉTATS-UNIS
OECD Publications and Information Centre,
2001 L Street, N.W., Suite 700,
Washington, D.C. 20036 - 4095
Tel. (202) 785.6323

VENEZUELA
Libreria del Este,
Avda F. Miranda 52, Aptdo. 60337,
Edificio Galipan, Caracas 106
Tel. 951.17.05/951.23.07/951.12.97

YUGOSLAVIA - YOUGOSLAVIE
Jugoslovenska Knjiga, Knez Mihajlova 2,
P.O.B. 36, Beograd   Tel. 621.992

Orders and inquiries from countries where
Distributors have not yet been appointed should be
sent to:
OECD, Publications Service, 2, rue André-Pascal,
75775 PARIS CEDEX 16.

Les commandes provenant de pays où l'OCDE n'a
pas encore désigné de distributeur doivent être
adressées à :
OCDE, Service des Publications. 2, rue André-
Pascal, 75775 PARIS CEDEX 16.

72380-1-1989

OECD PUBLICATIONS, 2, rue André-Pascal, 75775 PARIS CEDEX 16 - No. 44621 1989
PRINTED IN FRANCE
(96 89 01 1) ISBN 92-64-13195-7